A Letter to My Love

THE   NUMB. V.

BARBADOS-GAZETTE;

With the freshest Advices Foreign and Domestick.

Saturday, November the 6th, 1731. To be continued Weekly.

IT seems to me very odd and unaccountable that notwithstanding my declaring my self at my first setting out to be free from all Party-Disputes, and utterly to reject any Overtures that might be made me towards introducing Personal Reflections, that I should lie under the Imputation of both these Faults. But what I'm more particularly concern'd at is, I'm told the Ladies here think themselves struck at by my Prometheus Story [No. 2] 'Tis wonderful that they will take it into their Heads, to think that whilst Dr. Swift was writing to the good People of Ireland, by Way of Parable, that He should hook in the Ladies of this Island; or that I should be thought to introduce it with that View, who am not as yet well enough acquainted with any of them to know Whether they have any Faults at all; but am rather apt to think of 'em, as Mr. Pope does of his Belinda in the Rape of the Lock;

If to their Share some Female Errors fall;
Look on their Eyes, and you'll forget 'em all.

However I hope the following Piece cannot be disagreeable to the Fair, for whose Sakes I now insert it.

Tolle moras, semper nocuit differre paratis.
                                    LUCAN.

THE properest Time for a Woman to be marry'd, is, most certainly, when a good Husband offers. Such an Opportunity ought, by no Means, to be neglected, for fear it never shou'd return again: And, therefore, I cannot help being displeas'd at my Cousin HUMPHRY, who, lately, has rejected very honourable and generous Proposals for his youngest Daughter LUCY, made by a Gentleman, to whom there can be no just Exception: For, his Fortune is not only clear and easy, h's Age suitable to hers, his Person agreeable, and his Character such as very few now a-days can pretend to; but, what is more than all, he loves the Girl with an unfeigned Affection, as the fairness of his Proposals testify.

Toward the End of the last Summer, LUCY happen'd one Evening to be walking with some other Ladies in the Royal Gardens at Kensington; there the Gentleman I am speaking of, first saw her; and being extreamly taken with her Truth and Beauty, (for she was then about Eighteen, and might well enough be called handsom) he enquir'd who she was, and made it his Business to get into her Company; which, after some Time, he effected, by the Assistance of a Female Acquaintance, at whose House she used to visit; where coming in, as it were by Accident, he drank Tea with her, and found in her Conversation so much good Sense, intermixt with a lively Wit, and abundance of good Nature, that he resolv'd, from that very Hour to make her his Wife, if possible. After this, he went to every Place where he thought it likely that he might see her, and gaz'd upon her, whenever they met, with Eyes so full of Fondness and Delight, that he was soon convinc'd of her Conquest over him: for Love is able to express itself without the Help of Words.

As Women seldom are displeased to think themselves belov'd; and especially, when the Lover happens to be wealthy, young, and handsom, LUCY, you may imagine, was not at all dissatisfy'd with this Discovery; and as LEANDER (for so at present we will call him) watch'd every Opportunity to speak his Passion, it was not a great while before she gave him one, either by Design or Acci-

dent. Her Heart was hitherto entirely disengag'd, but not averse to Love: she had no Dislike to Matrimony tho', as yet, she had beheld all Mankind with a real Indifference; but when she heard LEANDER pressing for her an invincible Affection, in the softest Language that Love could Dictate, and saw him stand before her all pale and trembling, a Tenderness she ne'er had known before came over her, and she could not for her Life refuse to grant him a private Interview, which he with the utmost Earnestness requested.

Their Friend's House, where he first fell into her Company, was the Place appointed for this Meeting, and the Time the Sunday following, when (pretending to go to Church, and visit a Neighbour afterwards) she found him there, waiting with Impatience for her. His Joy to see her was inexpressible; he seiz'd her Hand, which he press'd closely to his Lips, and leading her to a Chair, seated himself by her, and fix'd his Eyes upon her, but was unable to speak a Word. Her Cousin was still greater, for it cover'd her Cheeks with Blushes, and she could not so much as look upon him, but appear'd senseless and immoveable; 'till, at last, awaking, as it were, from her silent Ecstasy, LEANDER thank'd her in the most passionate Manner, for her condescending Goodness, to one that could not live without her.

It is impossible to declare half the fond Things he said to her in the two Hours they stay'd together, but the Sum of all was, that he hoped she would accept his Services, and in Time consent to be his Wife, and, withal, that she would grant him another Meeting. LUCY's Heart was not Proof against the first Attacks, and began to melt with Pity, or Love, or both, and her real Sentiments were enough in LEANDER's Favour; However, she judg'd it highly proper to conceal them, and therefore told him, she was too sensible of the wrong Step she had already made, to think of doing so any more; and it indeed she had a good Opinion of her, she was disirous not to forfeit it; by coming into Appointments of that Nature: In short, that she durst not hear any farther Discourse upon this Subject, without her Father's Knowledge and Approbation.

LEANDER, whose Designs were fair and honourable, waited the next Day upon Cousin HUMPHRY, without being much afraid of a Refusal; because, as to Portion and Settlement, which are the Points Parents most commonly stick at, he was resolved there should be no Dispute between them. —— Sir, says LEANDER, you are not a Stranger to my Estate and Character, my present Business is, to beg that you'll permit my Addresses to your Daughter, for whom I have the most sincere Regard: As to Fortune, give her just what you please, and be assur'd she may command whatever is in my Power. Cousin HUMPHRY received him very civilly, having been long acquainted with LEANDER's Family, and knowing very well that himself was a Gentleman of undoubted Worth and Merit. Sir, says he, I am highly sensible of the Honour you do my Family; but pray, which of my three Daughters occasions me the Favour of this Visit? Miss LUCY, replies LEANDER, is the Object of all my Wishes, and the only can make me happy, Sir, says Cousin HUMPHRY, with much Earnestness, do you know she is my youngest Daughter, and that her Sisters are both unmarry'd? If you can like the Eldest, I will give her you with all my Heart, and shall be proud of such a Sin in Law; but I can act no otherwise, for Providence has pointed out in what Order I must dispose of them, and nothing is more plain, than that she who was first born, ought likewise to be first marry'd.

LEANDER was not a little surpriz'd at this unexpected objection, which, at first, he knew not what to make of, or how to take, whether in jest or earnest; but, upon farther Discourse, he found, to his exceeding Mortification, that it was my Cousin HUMPHRY's sixt Determination, and that all his Arguments and Persuasion to the contrary, signify'd just nothing. It was all in vain to urge, that
                                              his

The first page of the earliest surviving issue of the *Barbados Gazette,*
6 November 1731. Reproduced by permission of the British Library,
shelfmark Burney 289B.

A Letter to My Love

Love Poems by Women
First Published
in the *Barbados Gazette,*
1731–1737

Edited with an Introduction,
Afterword, and Notes by
Bill Overton

*To Ruth with best wishes
from Bill*

February 2002

DELAWARE

Newark: University of Delaware Press
London: Associated University Presses

Associated University Presses
440 Forsgate Drive
Cranbury, NJ 08512

Associated University Presses
16 Barter Street
London WC1A 2AH, England

Associated University Presses
P.O. Box 338, Port Credit
Mississauga, Ontario
Canada L5G 4L8

The paper used in this publication meets the requirements of the American National Standard for Permanence of Paper for Printed Library Materials Z39.48-1984.

Library of Congress Cataloging-in-Publication Data

A letter to my love : love poems by women first published in the Barbados gazette, 1731–1737 / edited with an introduction, afterword, and notes by Bill Overton.
    p.   cm.
Includes index.
ISBN 0-87413-746-2 (alk. paper)
    1. Love poetry, English.   2. English poetry—18th century.
3. English poetry—Women authors.   4. Sansom, Martha Fowke,
1689–1736—Authorship.   I. Overton, Bill.   II. Barbados gazette.
PR1184.L37   2001
821′.5—dc21   2001027013

Contents

Preface

Between July 1733 and March 1735, a series of twenty-six love poems appeared at irregular intervals in the *Barbados Gazette*, one of the earliest newspapers published regularly in the Caribbean. Neither author nor addressee was named; but the poems had been written by a lady in London some years previously, and the addressee was a gentleman who for at least seven years had been living in Barbados. According to the newspaper's editor, Samuel Keimer, the poems had come from a third party, and were printed on condition that identities be concealed. Keimer claimed, however, that the lady had been well known in English society; and he printed a letter from his anonymous informant which intimated that at some future date the reasons for secrecy might be revealed.

Since very few issues of the *Barbados Gazette* survive, none of which contain any of the poems,[1] they would have sunk into oblivion, along with much other interesting material, had it not been for two key initiatives. First, a selection of items printed during the paper's first seven years was published in London in 1741. Entitled *Caribbeana*, this anthology consists of two handsome octavo volumes; it is the only known primary source for the twenty-six poems, and for much else.[2] Second, much more recently, Roger Lonsdale included three of the poems in *Eighteenth-Century Women Poets: An Oxford Anthology*, the second of his two ground-breaking collections of eighteenth-century verse.[3] Taking a cue from one of the adjectives applied to the writer of the poems by Keimer, Lonsdale avoided the lonely label "anonymous" by calling her "the amorous lady."

Lonsdale's two collections, founded on nothing less than a thorough reading and reassessment of virtually all the verse extant from the period, open up many fresh discoveries, and, in doing so, go far towards redefining the eighteenth-century poetic canon. Among the most exciting finds are the poems included in

7

the present edition. The poems are important because they are part of a submerged continent of women's achievement which researchers are bringing to light, and because, like other discoveries in the field of eighteenth-century verse, they challenge many stock assumptions about it. The most powerful argument for their significance is, however, their quality. I believe that they are not only the best love poems of their period, but that some of them stand comparison with the best English love poems of any period, not excluding Shakespeare's; and that, taken together, they constitute a series that deserves to be known as well as the love lyrics of Donne, or Hardy's *Poems of 1912–13*. If such claims sound extravagant, they can be tested from this edition, the chief purpose of which is to help get these extraordinary poems known.

Samuel Keimer, who first published the poems, never redeemed the hint that the reasons for concealing the identities of author and addressee might be revealed, and much else remains mysterious. But the poems by the so-called "amorous lady" are not the only verse to appear in *Caribbeana*; more especially, they are not its only female-authored love poems. The collection also includes fourteen further anonymous poems of this kind, and one poem by a woman under the pseudonym Clio to an unnamed man whose verse she admired. Unlike the poems attributed to the "amorous lady," and except for five poems printed in a single issue of the paper, all but the last of these items appeared one by one and with little or no indication of authorship. However, Clio was the pen name of Martha Fowke, and Phyllis J. Guskin has argued that it is to Fowke that all of the poems should be assigned. Guskin proposed her claim in a 1993 conference paper, a revised version of which is to appear in a forthcoming issue of *Eighteenth-Century Studies*; and she restated it in her edition of *Clio*, the autobiography-cum-apologia-cum-extended-love-letter addressed in 1723 by Fowke to Aaron Hill.[4] In several ways the evidence she provides is persuasive, but it does not yet afford definitive proof either that the so-called "amorous lady" and the writer of the other fifteen poems are one and the same, or that she was Martha Fowke. I hope this edition will stimulate further research on questions of authorship, especially because it may not only help to identify positively the writer or writers of the poems, but lead to the finding of more of her or their work.

The question of identification also has a further side to it. Keimer referred to the writer of the twenty-six anonymous love poems by a variety of phrases, mostly tendentious, and including "the amorous Fair one" (1:264), "the *amorous* Lady" (1:314), "the ingenious Lady" (1:360), "the amorous Heroine" (1:366), and "the same *Female Wit*" (2:29). Because these designations appeal to stereotypes of gender roles which emphasize sex, in some cases in both senses of the word, more than poetry, I believe it is best to discard the soubriquet adapted by Lonsdale from Keimer. It is possible that future research will enable the poems to be attributed definitively to Martha Fowke, or to another named author. Until either breakthrough occurs, I prefer to call her "the anonymous lady."

In order to enable comparison between the twenty-six poems assigned to the anonymous lady and the other anonymous female-authored love poems published in *Caribbeana*, this edition prints all of them. For the same reason, and to provide further evidence for testing Guskin's claim that all forty-one are by Martha Fowke, it also includes two of the latter's poems. One of these is the poem which bears her pen name Clio; the other is from the eponymous memoir which she wrote for Aaron Hill. Thirdly, and again to provide as much evidence as possible in the available space, this edition also reprints all of the prefatory information to the poems given in *Caribbeana*. I hope readers will find not only much to admire and enjoy in the verse, but also enough other material to follow up some of the many questions it raises.

Acknowledgments

T HIS EDITION COULD NOT HAVE BEEN COMPLETED WITHOUT VERY considerable help both from institutions and from individuals. I am indebted to Loughborough University for granting me a semester's study leave during which I was able to bring it to completion, and to colleagues in the Department of English and Drama, especially Marion Shaw, for their interest and backing. I also wish to express my great appreciation of the facilities and assistance provided by staff at the Pilkington Library of Loughborough University; the British Library; Cambridge University Library; the Bodleian Library; the libraries of Nottingham, Leicester, and London Universities; the Brotherton Collection at Leeds University; and at the Leicestershire Record Office. I am indebted, too, to staff at Lambeth Palace Library and the New York Public Library for locating and sending me copies of early issues of the *Barbados Gazette*; and to Donald Salt at the Leicester Cathedral Office for information about Martha Fowke's memorial tablet.

Other individuals who have given help, and to whom I am especially grateful, are Phyllis Guskin, who has generously shared with me her research on the attribution of the poems, sending me a copy of her conference paper on the subject and her forthcoming article in *Eighteenth-Century Studies*, and who commented on my first draft; Isobel Grundy, who discussed the poems of the anonymous lady with me, encouraged me to produce this edition, and gave me access to a copy of *Caribbeana*; Warren Chernaik, Christine Gerrard, Robin Hamilton and Calhoun Winton, who responded to enquiries about Waller, the Hill circle, Dryden, and Addison and Steele respectively; Gill Spraggs, who commented on the poems, advised on classical literature, especially Sappho, and discovered a set of allusions to a passage from Virgil's *Aeneid*; Martha Davis, Virginia Knight, and other members of the Classics email discussion list located at

11

the University of Washington, Seattle, who helped answer queries arising from further classical allusions; Chris White, who advised on possible illustrations for the cover; and participants in the seminar on Attribution and Anonymity in Eighteenth-Century Writing at the biennial conference of the Council for College and University English, held in September 1998 at Loughborough University, who discussed early drafts of parts of the Introduction and Afterword.

Finally, the edition has benefited from the comments of Keith Overton, who also read it in draft; from the companionship of George Overton, Henry Overton, Julie Page and Sally Andreasen, who did their best to keep me sane while I was working on it; advice and support of the Managing Editor of Associated University Presses, Christine Retz; and, above all, from the help, advice and support of Elaine Hobby. Where it has failed to profit from the advice and assistance I have received, the fault is mine.

Note on the Texts

ALL POEMS AND PROSE ARE PRESENTED IN UNMODERNIZED FORM, with the original spelling, punctuation, italics, and capitalization, because this presents no significant hindrance to comprehension. However, the initial capital for the first word of each poem is silently normalized from large to standard-size font; where whole words are set in capitals at the beginnings of poems, stanzas, and of prose paragraphs, lower case is used instead, except for the first word's initial letter; where a whole poem or prose passage is printed in italics, this is changed to roman, and the change is recorded in Appendix A or the endnotes; long "s" is amended to short; and, in discussion of the poems in the Introduction and Afterword, their titles are cited in modernized form. All the poems from *Caribbeana* included in the edition are numbered consecutively to enable identification, because some lack titles and others—for example, those headed "To the Same"—carry titles which do not allow them to be distinguished.

Nearly all the verse and prose quoted or cited was published before 1752, when Britain and its colonies still observed the Julian calendar, and the New Year was traditionally dated from March 25—as it was in the *Barbados Gazette*, though not always consistently elsewhere. To avoid confusion, this edition amends the year where necessary to conform with modern usage.

Another possible source of confusion is over the name of the author to whom Phyllis Guskin has attributed all of the poems from *Caribbeana* printed in this edition. Since most of these poems, if they are by Fowke, were written before her marriage, and since she is not known to have published under her married name of Sansom, this edition refers to her throughout as Martha Fowke.

Introduction

THE BARBADOS GAZETTE

ALTHOUGH NOT THE FIRST CARIBBEAN NEWSPAPER—AN HONOR BE-
longing to the *Weekly Jamaica Courant,* first issued in 1718—the
Barbados Gazette was the first newspaper "known to have been
published twice a week, for any considerable time, in any part of
America."[1] It was founded by Samuel Keimer, at first as a weekly;
according to E. M. Shilstone's deductions, its opening number
appeared on Saturday 9 October 1731.[2]

Keimer had led a colorful life in London and Philadelphia. As
he had recorded in the narrative of his religious conversion, *A
Brand Pluck'd from the Burning,* in London he had trained as a
printer, joined a group of religious enthusiasts, and fallen foul of
the laws for debt and seditious libel.[3] In Philadelphia he em-
ployed Benjamin Franklin in the printing press he had set up
there, but he was a poor businessman. When Franklin became a
printer in his own right, Keimer tried to forestall him in setting
up a newspaper, which he styled *The Universal Instructor in All
Arts and Sciences; And Pennsylvania Gazette.* The instruction
flourished by the title consisted chiefly of extracts from Ephraim
Chambers's *Cyclopedia,* just published in London, and instal-
ments from Defoe's *Religious Courtship.*[4] Not surprisingly,
Keimer's venture misfired, and he sold the paper to his rival. Re-
launched by Franklin and his partner, and shorn of the over-
weening part of its title, it proved a famous success as the *Penn-
sylvania Gazette.*[5]

According to Franklin, Keimer was "at last forc'd to sell his
Printing-house to satisfy his Creditors" and went to Barbados.[6]
There he was joined by another former employee, David Harry,
who brought with him the island's first printing press. When Har-
ry's business failed, mounting debts forced him to sell the press
and return to Philadelphia. It is not clear whether Keimer him-
self was the buyer. Franklin says he was not, but that he was em-

ployed to run the press by an unnamed purchaser; while Isaiah
Thomas states that Keimer "found friends to assist him in the
purchase."[7] It seems unlikely that the ever-impecunious Keimer
could have raised the money himself, and the *Barbados Gazette*
is a striking enough improvement on his first attempt to suggest
that he had not only learned from Franklin's example but also
obtained help with the contents. Like the relaunched *Pennsylva-
nia Gazette*, the new paper combined news items with others of
social, literary, and cultural interest—including, in particular,
verse. Within nine months it was able to expand to twice-weekly
publication, on Wednesdays as well as on Saturdays, and Keimer
continued publishing it for over seven years, after which, and de-
spite competition from rival papers, it kept on until at least 1797.[8]
What distinguished the *Barbados Gazette* during Keimer's edi-
torship was its success at integrating the normal functions of a
colonial newspaper at the time with the appeal of a miscellane-
ous journal. The more general material it published—essays on
topical subjects as well as poems—was to lend itself especially to
reprinting in *Caribbeana*.

The Barbados Gazette and Caribbeana

Only five issues of the *Barbados Gazette* dating from the 1730s
appear to survive: one in the Burney Collection at the British Li-
brary, one in the New York Public Library, and three in Lambeth
Palace Library. The one in the Burney Collection, the earliest of
the five, consists of four pages printed in two columns.[9] It con-
tains an exemplary story of love and marriage, clearly in emula-
tion of the *Spectator* and occupying most of the first page and
nearly half of the second; a section of news from abroad, half
from Continental Europe and half from Britain, filling the rest of
the second page and most of the third; a small section of news
from Barbados, chiefly about shipping; and, on the last page, two
poems, taking up one and a half columns, followed by three ad-
vertisements. The first poem, "On Celia. Epigram," is given in
Caribbeana not under the actual date of the issue, 6 November
1731, but as if it had been part of the issue for 11 December. This
anomaly is explained in the Preface to the anthology, which
states that some items which "had no Relation to Dates are re-

moved from the Places they originally held, for the Sake of lengthening some Papers which might otherwise look too short" (1:ix). The second poem, "The Quack-Doctor," is a broad tale in hudibrastic verse. It does not appear in *Caribbeana*, perhaps because the compiler thought it too crude.

None of the remaining issues to survive from the 1730s contains any poems, and, unlike the one in the Burney Collection, each consists only of two pages of two columns. Three and a half columns of the one in the New York Public Library, for 18 April 1733, are taken up with addresses given by the new Governor, Lord Howe, to the island's Council and Assembly, and by the King a few months earlier to Parliament. The Governor's address, included in *Caribbeana* (1:139–41), apologizes for his delay in arriving, sets out his immediate aims, and, declaring his concern for the island's prosperity, pledges his determination to promote it. The King's speech, which is rather shorter, exhorts Parliament "to give all possible Dispatch to the Publick Business" which his ministers are to introduce in the current year. Neither it nor the news item and announcement which follow is reprinted in *Caribbeana*; instead, a poem is inserted, again presumably from an issue of another date, celebrating the new Governor's arrival. Lord Howe, who died suddenly after only two years in office, is also the chief subject of the issues in Lambeth Palace Library, dated 29 March, 9 April, and 3 May 1735. These are all tributes to his memory, and all are represented in *Caribbeana*, again without the news items or advertisements (2:38–40, 40–43, 58–62). Since, unlike the early issue in the Burney Collection, the four other issues of the *Gazette* to survive from the 1730s consist only of two pages, it is possible either that Keimer switched to this format when he began to produce his paper twice a week, or that on occasion he varied its length according to the material at hand. Isaiah Thomas says that Keimer continued to publish the *Gazette* "until the end of 1738," at which time he seems to have sold his press to William Beeby, who carried on producing the paper from the same address.[10] The sale helps explain why the material reprinted in *Caribbeana* ends in the same year—the last number included is dated 16 December.

Though most reference sources credit Keimer with editing *Caribbeana*, three facts suggest otherwise. First, the Prefaces to the two volumes, which are unsigned, are dated from Gray's Inn

in London; second, Keimer died in Barbados not long afterwards;
third, he is unlikely to have possessed the detailed legal and his-
torical knowledge reflected especially in the second Preface.[11]
While it is possible that Keimer had some role in the publication,
even if only that of collecting issues for reprinting, it is more
likely that, as Phyllis J. Guskin has argued, the compiler and per-
haps also the author of the two Prefaces was Jonathan Blenman,
Attorney-General of Barbados.[12] As I will show below, there are
clear indications that Blenman contributed to the *Barbados Ga-
zette*, and external evidence as well as two footnotes in the text
(1:269, 402) attest to his presence in London at the time *Caribbe-
ana* would have been in press.

    Caribbeana selects from the *Barbados Gazette* both in repre-
senting some issues and not others, and in representing issues
only in part. For example, the numbers that survive make clear
that news of passing or local interest was omitted. A further re-
mark in the Preface draws attention to omissions of this kind:

> the Printer, who was the first Projector of a News-Paper in *Barba-
> dos*, having set out on a very narrow Bottom, his *Gazette* towards
> the Beginning seldom yielded any Thing worthy of transcribing; and
> accordingly there will appear large Chasms at first especially, and
> often indeed throughout, betwixt the respective Dates of some of
> those we have taken which, though there must necessarily be now
> and then a Want of Connexion, are, however, all ranged in due Order
> of Time. (1:ix)

It is therefore difficult to form a wholly accurate idea of the *Ga-
zette*, especially because not every item was printed in the issue
to which the compiler assigned it. Nevertheless, it is possible to
glean from *Caribbeana* information of various kinds which is im-
portant to an understanding both of the poems reprinted in this
edition and of the social and historical circumstances of their
first publication.

    In keeping with the prefatory remark just quoted about gaps
in the issues included, the first number represented in *Caribbe-
ana* is dated Saturday, 20 November 1731, seven weeks after the
paper had started. Twice-weekly publication seems to have
begun on 8 August 1732, the first Wednesday issue represented,
and apparently number forty-five. As already stated, the final

number included in *Caribbeana* is dated 16 December 1738. Assuming continuous publication, over seven hundred numbers must have appeared by that point, and extracts from 166 of these are represented.

Bearing all this in mind, the selection of issues, and the distribution among them of items of verse, are particularly significant. Two main patterns may be discerned. First, most of the issues included occur in a three-year period extending from the summer of 1732 to the summer of 1735. The representation of issues from Fall 1731, when the *Gazette* began, to Summer 1732 is patchy, as might be expected given that the venture took time to find its feet; and after the summer of 1735 there are several gaps of two months or more, and in two cases for periods of over four months.[13] The second main pattern is that the three-year period from which the largest number of issues was selected for *Caribbeana* is also the period in which most of the verse, and more especially the love poetry, was published. In one way this is scarcely surprising, because the compiler would have been well aware that literary material, and general material on commercial, legal, or political topics, would have appealed best to readers in the 1740s. What this does not explain, however, is why the proportion of literary material, and particularly of love poems, declined so markedly after the summer of 1735. I will return to this question below, but first it is important to gain an idea of what kind of verse appeared in the *Gazette*. This information is available only from *Caribbeana*, because the sole surviving issue to contain verse is the one in the Burney Collection described above.

The verse in *Caribbeana*

For the reasons just explained, the proportion of verse selected for inclusion in the compilation is likely to have been high. Between them, the 166 issues of the *Barbados Gazette* represented in *Caribbeana* include no fewer than 140 items of original verse. These items appeared in ninety-one of the 166 issues, some of them in groups of up to six at a time. The range of verse included is quite wide. At one end of the spectrum are epigrams, of which there are thirty-eight. It is not surprising to find this kind of verse figuring so prominently, since it was popular at the period, especially in magazines, and since it often inspired readers to send in attempts of their own. In a similar class are other slight humorous pieces, including riddles and satirical squibs, and also social or complimentary verse, such as "To Miss * * * * * *, on her Dancing at Mr. Frith's Ball in Bridge-Town, December 18, 1732" (1:102) and "The Barbados Beauties" (2:277–78). At the opposite end of the spectrum there are various examples of serious formal verse. These include prologues and epilogues (two of each); translations (four—three of them from the Bible); classical imitations (three); poems of tribute (six, among them three to the newly appointed Governor Howe); elegies (two, including one on Governor Howe's sudden death); epitaphs (two); and two poems of moral and religious reflection, one in English and one in Latin. Four other poems are also in Latin, though two of these are humorous; there are two vernacular prayers; and there is a solitary example each of a religio-scientific poem, a pastoral lyric, and a fable.

This impressive range of material is fairly characteristic of poetry miscellanies at the time.[14] What is most striking about it, however, is the large size of a category of verse not mentioned so far in this analysis. Though the distinctions between one kind of poem and another are not always easy to draw, over a third of the items may be classed as love poems—forty-nine of the total of 140. Of these, nine are attributed to or were patently written by men, but the great majority are attributed to or appear to have been written by women. While some of the love poems by men are accomplished, they are all to a greater or lesser extent conventional; so, with one exception, I will say no more of them here. The total of forty love poems by women include twenty-six assigned to the anonymous lady. The remaining fourteen include some with introductions giving further information, others specifying the writer's sex but little else, and others still with no introduction at all. Although men sometimes used a female persona, there is no evidence that any of the poems attributed to women are of male authorship. The same applies to the three poems accompanied by no indication of the author's sex, all of which appear on internal evidence to have been written by women.[15]

Of the fourteen female-authored love poems not assigned to the anonymous lady, five were published together in a single issue, for 25 April 1733, and are said to be early poems by a young woman whose later verse was admired. The remaining nine poems appear at irregular intervals, with no indication of authorship, and in most cases without introduction. The poems assigned to the anonymous lady are the only ones of the forty to constitute a series, though an intermittent one, spread over more than a single issue. This distinction has special implications for the problem of attribution.

The distribution of the anonymous love poems by women is complex and difficult to interpret. The first appears in a very early issue, for 18 December 1731, without any kind of preliminary. It is followed in June 1732 by a longer poem, "Written at Midnight," which Keimer claims was "never before in print, tho' wrote many Years ago," and which he summarizes as "the tender Lamentation of a fair Lady, on being disappointed of suitable Returns to her Passion" (1:26); and then, in December of the same year, by another poem without any introduction, entitled "To * * * * * * * *." Next, in April 1733, appears the group of five poems just mentioned; and this is followed, at the end of June, by a poem entitled "An Imitation of Sappho." It is only after this, in July 1733, that the first item assigned to the anonymous lady appears; but then a gap of four months intervenes before there are any further love poems by women: three ascribed to the anonymous lady in the issue for 28 November. The next year, 1734, sees the largest number of poems attributed to the anonymous lady, and indeed the largest number of love poems—twenty-four, all by women—in any of the years covered by *Caribbeana*. This cluster begins in the first issue of the year with "On Christmas Morning," another of the poems ascribed to an unidentified woman, but the next fourteen love poems are all assigned to the anonymous lady. They occur in instalments of four, six, and four poems respectively, in three issues of February to March. The remaining six poems by the anonymous lady published in 1734 appeared one by one in separate issues, except for the last two, printed together on 9 November. They are interspersed with three other female-authored anonymous love poems, in the issues for 30 March, 17 August, and 19 October. The final two poems by the anonymous lady appear in a single issue, for 1 March, 1735; and after this only one further love poem attributed to a woman is included, a pastoral lyric in an issue of January 1737.

Two facts about the distribution of the poems are especially interesting. First, most of them were published between April 1733 and November 1734; second, after the appearance in March 1735 of the last two poems assigned to the anonymous lady, only one love poem by a woman is included, the pastoral lyric published nearly two years later. The virtual disappearance of love poems from *Caribbeana* after the issue for 1 March 1735 is to some extent in keeping with the decline noted above in the number of issues included and in the representation of verse of all kinds. After that date, only thirty-six poems appear. All are thoroughly conventional, and no fewer than seventeen are examples of that slight though diverting form of verse, the epigram.

I suggest three possible ways of accounting for the decrease in verse items and the near-absence of amatory verse after March 1735. First, it is likely that Keimer had only a limited stock of such items at his disposal, and that it simply ran out. In keeping with this hypothesis is the fact that the number of poems written in Barbados rather than in England increased as the *Gazette* continued. Although the place of composition is not always given, over half of the verse printed across the run of issues included in *Caribbeana* was clearly composed on the island, but after March 1735 this proportion further rises. Second, it may be that the one or more correspondents who, according to Keimer, provided him with the poems of the anonymous lady and with other verse withheld further supplies. The final issue to contain poems assigned to the anonymous lady is prefaced by an attempt to dispel a possible implication in one of these poems that there was "a *Criminal* Amour betwixt the Parties" (2:29). Perhaps the fear of scandal led the supplier of the manuscripts to insist that no more be published. Third, if there were grounds for such a fear, it is also conceivable that by this time amatory verse was itself regarded as less suitable for inclusion in the newspaper. This would be consistent with the fact that, whereas there are occasional racy or even mildly bawdy items in issues represented before the spring of 1735, very few sound this kind of note afterwards.

AUTHORS, CONTRIBUTORS, AND EDITORSHIP

Evidence concerning how Keimer came by the verse originally written in England is limited. As already mentioned, some poems were printed without introduction; and, because no relevant copies of the *Gazette* have survived, there is no knowing whether it gave details omitted in *Caribbeana*. Where provenance is indicated, credit is usually given to a friend of the editor, formerly in London but now on the island. Even this pattern, however, is not consistent. For example, although some of the poems by the anonymous lady, including the first, are introduced in the form of a letter from a correspondent, others appear direct from Keimer, sometimes under the heading "From my Chapel" (meaning his printing-room); and two state explicitly that the poems came to him via an intermediary (1:264, 2:29). This apparent arbitrariness may have been the result of negligence, or part of a deliberate attempt at a smokescreen to conceal the source. However, there are clearer indications of provenance for some of the verse in *Caribbeana* that required less discretion. In particular, it is likely that one of the key suppliers was the man who may also have edited the anthology, Jonathan Blenman.

Appointed Attorney-General in 1726 and Judge of the Vice-Admiralty Court eight years later, Blenman enjoyed a long and at times turbulent career in Barbados.[16] A keen controversialist, he published several pamphlets, including two as a young man, on political, legal, and colonial questions.[17] The most direct evidence for Blenman's involvement with the *Gazette* is a poem which appears to have been written to him about ten years previously. Keimer's introduction begins by stating: "The following *Epistolary Poem* was wrote some Years ago, by a noted *Scots Bard*, (still living) whilst he was then in *Lymbo*, to an Acquaintance of his, now in this Island" (1:54). The poem, which is a witty appeal for help in getting out of debtors' prison, is headed "To ********
*******, Esq;," it is dated "*Jan.* 4, 1721," and it is initialled "J. M." A footnote in *Caribbeana* adds that the writer "is since dead, and these Lines no where else to be found." As Phyllis Guskin has pointed out, the writer was Joseph Mitchell (1684–1738), and the number of asterisks in the title matches the number of letters in Jonathan Blenman's name;[18] indeed the poem gives further hints, as it begins by addressing "B******," again with the right number of asterisks, and refers to his occupation as a lawyer.

There is, next, some basis for speculating that Blenman may have supplied Keimer with a number of poems written in London in about 1715–17. At this period he was on the threshold of his legal career, and the friendship indicated by Joseph Mitchell's poem suggests that he also had literary interests—if, as seems almost certain, he was its addressee. The first example is a courtship poem addressed to the recently widowed Elizabeth Rowe, printed in *Caribbeana* with her scornful reply (1:112–13). These poems are not otherwise known to have been published before 1739, when, following Rowe's death, they appeared in her *Miscellaneous Works*; and both have significantly different titles.[19] The letter introducing them claims not only that the two poems had not appeared before, "altho' wrote near seventeen Years ago," but that the one to Rowe was written "by a Gentleman, who is now, and has been for the greatest Part of that Time, in this Island" (1:111). Blenman may conceivably have tried to advance his social and literary ambitions by an address to a lady who was not only well known for her verse but who, like him, was a Nonconformist from Somerset.[20]

Two other poems possibly provided by Blenman are connected with the theater. The first is a short piece of occasional verse by the dramatist Susanna Centlivre. According to Keimer, its ten lines were "never before in Print," and were written "*extempore*, by the celebrated Female Poet whose Name they bear, in a Letter to a Person of known Generosity (now residing here) on Occasion of a new Play of the Author's, which was to be acted the same Evening, for her Benefit" (1:48). The other is an occasional poem entitled "To Mr. *Keen* on the New Play-House" (1:380–81), clearly referring to the defection of the actor Theophilus Keene to John Rich's new playhouse in Lincoln's Inn Fields, where he first appeared on 4 January 1715.[21] The introduction to this poem, at the end of a letter signed "Philalethes," attributes it to "an Acquaintance," and claims that it was "wrote many Years ago, when the Author was very young," and, once more, that it had not been published previously.

Lastly, it is probable that Blenman or an associate of his in England or Barbados wrote a panegyric entitled "To Mr. -------- on his Incomparable Lines," in praise of a verse tribute to the Duke of Marlborough that seems to have been addressed to Addison (1:358–60). Keimer's introduction ends by remarking: "The Poem was wrote several Years ago, but has been kept ever since in Manuscript with many more, some whereof have already appear'd in the *Barbados-Gazette*; and this will probably, in due

Time, be follow'd by others no less worthy of it." It is possible that the tribute to which the poem refers is Addison's *The Campaign* (1705), but the word "Lines" in its title seems to indicate a shorter composition, perhaps "To his Grace the Duke of Marlborough, on the Report of his Going into Germany," probably by George Sewell, though sometimes attributed to Addison, and written in 1712 after the Duke had left the country to avoid charges of corruption.[22] The Whig politics of the poem in *Caribbeana* are consistent with Blenman's stance in his pamphlets of 1715 and 1717 as a Dissenter and a Hanoverian.

Other kinds of evidence also connect Blenman with the *Gazette*. First, the paper favored his position as Attorney-General in a long-running controversy over the payment of tax arrears. Second, although it is not possible to identify all of the items contributed by Blenman, among them were certainly five articles, later reprinted as a pamphlet in London, concerning the trial in New York of John Peter Zenger. The trial, which took place in 1736, resulted in a famous victory for press freedom, and also raised questions about the limits of British colonial jurisdiction. Blenman's authorship of the articles is further borne out by the manuscript inscription of his name on the title page of a 1770 reprint in the Library of Congress.[23] Third, *Remarks on Several Acts of Parliament*, published anonymously in 1742 but definitely by Blenman, quotes from and contains an advertisement for *Caribbeana*. Indeed, this book, along with a pamphlet published in 1740, also shows that Blenman was in London during the period in which both they and *Caribbeana* were published.[24]

The probability that Blenman not only contributed to the *Gazette* but had a hand in producing *Caribbeana* is therefore high. However, both the preface to volume 1 and the "Advertisement to the Reader" before the appendix to volume 2 suggest a need for caution in judging how far his involvement went. First, the preface ends by regretting that one man who had supplied material had withheld his help: "This Collection might, we are sensible, have appeared to more Advantage, if a *certain Gentleman*, now in these Parts (and whose Pen at first visibly contributed towards it) had been pleased to lend us his Assistance" (1:x). If the claim can be taken at face value, the words "at first" question whether this man could have been Blenman, whose "Remarks on *Zenger*'s Trial" were published as late as 1737 (2:198–221),

even though the phrase "in these Parts" indicates that he, like
Blenman, was in London at the time. Since the editor goes on to
remark that this other contributor "had, no doubt, his own Rea-
sons for declining thereof, yet without opposing however, or dis-
couraging the Undertaking," it appears that at least one of
Keimer's suppliers had reservations about *Caribbeana*. Second,
while *Caribbeana* gives few or no details about the provenance
of most of the material it reprints, the appendix is more informa-
tive, providing a source of some kind for each of its eight items.
Two of the items had already been printed in Barbados; but the
source for two others is described as "a very intelligent Person,
who has, in some Measure, made up for the Disappointment we
met with, from the Gentleman alluded to at the End of our Pref-
ace to the first Volume" (2:297, 299). The remaining four items
are attributed to three different sources. Item two, a set of legal
opinions, is stated to have come from "a Merchant in the *City*,
who had them sent over to him from *Barbados*" (2:298); item
four, reasons for a proposed excise-bill amendment and a royal
order relating to it, from "a Gentleman who had the former from
one of the Committee appointed to draw them up"; item five from
the same source; and item six, a letter from a gentleman in Bar-
bados to his friend in England about some unusual legal proceed-
ings, "from the Hands of the very Person in *London*, who
received it directly from *Barbados*; and with this Restriction
only, that the Name of the Author should be concealed" (2:299).

All this suggests that determining the provenance of the vari-
ous items in *Caribbeana* is difficult, and that in some—perhaps
many—cases it may prove impossible. While Blenman certainly
wrote some items and almost certainly contributed others not of
his own authorship, many others also contributed, both directly
and otherwise. In particular, it is not possible to verify Guskin's
claim that Blenman edited the collection. Although Guskin ar-
gues that his role "seems clearly established by the dating of the
Prefaces from Gray's Inn in 1740–1," since his son "was admitted
to Gray's Inn that year," neither piece of evidence is valid. First,
the address given in the prefaces seems much more likely to be
that of Thomas Osborne, the bookseller named first on the title
page, who had his premises in Gray's Inn from 1738–1767.[25] Sec-
ond, the *Letter from a Gentleman at Barbados*, edited by Blen-
man, has a preface signed with his initials giving his address and

the date as "Lincoln's-Inn-Fields, March 10, 1740 [i.e. 1741]."[26] Third, the date of Timothy Blenman's admission to Gray's Inn is recorded as 22 January 1742, and it seems unlikely that he could have taken chambers there as early as 1740, especially since he only matriculated at Christ Church, Oxford, in December 1741.[27] Indeed, Blenman's presence in London from Fall 1739 till at least the middle of 1742 is partly explained by concern for the education of his two sons; his elder son, William, was admitted to the Middle Temple, to which Blenman himself had been admitted nearly thirty years earlier, on 29 September 1739.[28] Thus, as with much else concerning *Caribbeana*, definitive answers to the problems of editorship, provenance, and authorship are not easily found.

THE ANONYMOUS LADY AND HER ADDRESSEE

Caribbeana supplies only a few tantalizing details about the anonymous lady. The main ones are as follows: the poet was living in London at the time they were written, but was dead by 1740, the date of the first Preface (1:ix); she was well known in society (1:ix, 1:247); she was a precocious writer who composed one of her most striking poems, "On Being Charged with Writing Incorrectly," when she was no more than nineteen (1:314); the poems to her lover were written "above Twelve Years" before November 1733 (1:247); and she already had a reputation for her poetry, because some of it, though not the poems printed in *Caribbeana*, had been circulated and probably published, and had attracted admiration (1:ix, 1:264). Finally, the poems had been brought to Barbados by the addressee (1:ix), were in the poet's own handwriting (1:360, 2:6), and had not been written for publication (2:29).

The evidence concerning the addressee is more limited. Keimer states that by June 1734 he had been in Barbados for "at least seven Years" (1:335), that he was "now, it seems, a Man of Business" (1:264), that he also wrote verse (1:335, 1:366), and that he had been less acceptable to the poet's relations than another suitor (2:29). Only the second of these details seems to add anything material, since the lover's residence in Barbados for more than seven years is not inconsistent with the writing of the poems over twelve years earlier, since the fact that he also wrote verse is apparent from poems 20 and 22, and since the existence of other suitors is presented as an inference. However, the reference to his profession is more useful. The probable sense is "One engaged in mercantile transactions," the first example of which dates from 1712 (*Oxford English Dictionary*). Although Guskin assumes that the phrase means "lawyer,"[29] this is unlikely, as the first example for the sense "The professional agent who transacts a person's legal business, an attorney," dates only from 1861.

The verse itself provides some further evidence, and, though this is slender, it has special importance in the absence of any other testimony. Several of the poems confirm that the writer had already made a name for herself as a poet; and one refers to the South Sea Bubble crash of Fall 1720, so corroborating the date of the love affair ("The Absent," line 23). Two other poems, 17, "To the Same," and 25, "To My Love," indicate that she had suitors; and a further two, which represent the name by which her lover addressed her with a dash, make it possible to infer that it had two syllables, because these are required by the meter in line 16 of poem 24, "To My Love. Wrote in Tears," and in line 11 of poem 26, "To the Same." On the same basis, line 20 of poem 16, "To the Same," and line 24 of poem 12, "The Absent," if it does not refer to the poet rather than her lover, suggest that the name by which she addressed him was also disyllabic.[30] Lastly, it seems that the lover may have been rather younger than the poet, since she addresses him as "my lovely Boy" in poem 3 (line 18) and as "my lovely Youth" in poem 23 (line 24), and, in poem 10, refers to his "giddy Youth" (line 17).

Phyllis Guskin presents several arguments for connecting what *Caribbeana* says about the anonymous lady with Martha Fowke. First, Fowke is the only known writer of the period who fits the details given: she had "made a considerable Figure in the *Beau Monde* at Home" (1:247); allowing for some exaggeration, she could be claimed to have "long since distinguished herself amongst the finest Writers in Poetry" (1:264); and she was dead by the time the preface to volume 1 of *Caribbeana* was written in 1740 (1:ix).[31] Born in 1689, Fowke was well known in the 1720s as a member of the circle around Aaron Hill. She was a precocious poet, as she points out in *Clio*, the lover's memoir she addressed to Hill, and as the epitaph by her brother confirms.[32] Guskin has discovered what seem to be the first poems published under Fowke's own name in a short-lived monthly, *Delights for the Ingenious*, which appeared during 1711; Fowke is commended in Giles Jacob's *Historical Account of the Lives and Writings of our Most Considerable English Poets* in 1720 and the same author's *Human Happiness* in the following year; and her verse is represented in various publications of the same decade, including *The Epistles of Clio and Strephon*, an exchange of platonic love letters, mostly in verse, written with William Bond and published in 1720, and miscellanies published by Anthony Hammond in the same year and by Richard Savage in 1726.[33]

Fowke also included forty poems and verse fragments in the lover's memoir mentioned above which Guskin has edited. Entitled *Clio: or, a Secret History of the Life and Amours of the Late Celebrated Mrs. S——N——M*, presumably by Hill's literary executors, this is dated 1723 but it was not published till 1752, two years after his death and sixteen after hers. Parts of *Clio* appear to respond to attacks on Fowke by Eliza Haywood to which the latter gave published expression in her scandal-novel of 1725–26, *Memoirs of a Certain Island Adjacent to the Kingdom of Utopia*.[34] If the anonymous lady was Martha Fowke, such notoriety lends color to Keimer's remark, quoted above, that she had "made a considerable Figure in the *Beau Monde* at home," and suggests why it might have been important to keep her identity secret. The fact that Fowke wrote so much amatory verse further strengthens Guskin's case for identifying her with the anonymous lady. If the identification is correct, it also casts additional light on the word "amorous" applied to her by Keimer and his correspondent. Other possible evidence for connecting Fowke with the anonymous lady is that Fowke's first name has the two syllables required by the meter of poems 24 and 26, as does her pseudonym Clio and her familiar name Patty.[35]

A second part of Guskin's argument for attributing the poems of the anonymous lady to Martha Fowke concerns the possible identity of their addressee and the circumstances in which they may have been written. In the 1993 conference paper in which she first proposed the attribution to Fowke, and also in *Clio* (p. 166), Guskin suggested that the addressee might have been Jonathan Blenman. In her article for *Eighteenth-Century Studies*, however, and following correspondence with myself, she puts forward a different candidate, an associate of Blenman called Nicholas Hope.[36] This is the person she believes to be the "Mr. *H*——" mentioned by Fowke in *Clio* as a young gentleman with whom she was in love but who had to leave England shortly after she married Arnold Sansom (*Clio*, pp. 128–31). In support of her case, Guskin points out that Blenman and Hope were in London in 1720. They had gone there with the Rector of St Michael's in Barbados, William Gordon, to protest at their oppression by the island's Governor, Robert Lowther. Entries in the *Calendar of State Papers (Colonial)* show that Hope was Gordon's attorney and that Blenman was counsel for another complainant, Francis Lansa. The three fled the island for redress in late 1719 or early 1720. A bill of indictment was found against Blenman on 29 March 1720, but by then they were in London, where he and Hope met the Secretary to the Council of Trade and Plantations on the following day.[37] Their mission proved entirely successful, for Lowther returned to London where he was deprived of his office. A pamphlet published in London in the same year containing copies of two letters by Blenman, and of the document committing him for trial, gives further evidence.[38]

According to Guskin, the "decisive clue" linking Martha Fowke to Blenman and Hope is a complimentary poem in *Caribbeana* dated 1720 and entitled "To the Reverend Mr. *Gordon*, on his Success in the Complaints against the late Governor of *Barbados*" (1:269–71). The poem is introduced by a paragraph explaining the circumstances of Gordon's mission, and this is amplified by a long footnote naming his companions. Internal evidence makes it clear that the poet was a woman in England, and Guskin argues that she was probably Fowke. Although this is by no means implausible, neither the poem nor the material accompanying it provides further evidence. However, the only specific indication the poems give for their date of composition is the reference to the South Sea Bubble crash of Fall 1720,[39] and there are reasons for doubting whether Blenman or Hope stayed in England as long as this. First, *Caribbeana* records that Blenman obtained an order from the Lords Justices dated 2 April 1720, in which the Governor was "declared *to have acted arbitrarily and illegally*" (1:269–70). Abel Boyer reports this as confirmed on 2 August in his *Political State of Great Britain*.[40] Second, a document signed by Blenman and other gentlemen of Barbados indicates that he must have been back on the island by late summer or early fall, because it refers to Lowther's departure, which had taken place on 30 June, and it was read by the Council on 7 December 1720.[41] There would have been no reason for Blenman to stay in London once his appeal had succeeded; indeed, *The Barbadoes Packet*, the Preface to which is dated 25 March 1720, declares that no one who considered the case fully would "attempt to hinder him from Hastening Home to his *Family*, which is now Languishing under a Thousand Perplexities and Apprehensions about him, and to his *Business and Affairs* which he was forc'd to leave in the utmost Disorder and Confusion."[42] Guskin claims that judgment was given "in August and October 1720," but the judgment dated 12 October—which Guskin cites from Schomburgk's *History of Barbados*, although Schomburgk gives *Caribbeana* as his source—concerns the proper jurisdiction of the court in Barbados rather than the appeal by Gordon or Blenman against Lowther; and a further item in Boyer, dated 13 October, refers to a quite different set of complaints.[43] The only other evidence concerning the length of time Blenman spent in London is ambiguous. It is the date 4 January 1721, given to the poem mentioned above that Joseph Mitchell addressed to him. Mitchell was a Scot, and, as Guskin explains, Scots had by long-standing custom dated the New Year from 1 January, unlike the English who until 1752 dated it from 25 March. The question is therefore whether Mitchell was following Scottish or English practice. If he was following Scottish practice, the 1721 date is correct, and this is significant because *Clio* indicates that Martha Fowke's "Mr. H——" was still in London in that year, at the time when Fowke apparently first met Aaron Hill.[44] If, however, Mitchell was following English practice, the "1721" of the poem would mean 1722, and this would suggest that Blenman returned to London, presumably on some other business. What is beyond doubt is that he and Hope went back to Barbados before Gordon, because he and his wife Mary had a son, William, baptized on 28 January 1722; a document in the *Calendar of State Papers* refers to fees charged by Hope in Barbados concerning a sloop seized "in March, 1721"; and the *Calendar* also records a letter from Gordon dated 15 June 1721, which "*Presses* for report upon the two Acts of Barbados concerning him, he being anxious to return

thither and the merchant ship for that Island sailing this week."
Whether or not this appeal succeeded, Gordon was back in Bar-
bados seven months later, on 28 January 1722, for he was one of
William Blenman's godfathers.[45]

However, even if Blenman and Hope were in London in early
1721, neither seems likely to have been the addressee of the
anonymous lady's poems. Guskin's original speculation that
Blenman might have been the addressee was based on the possi-
bility that the initial "H" in *Clio* was a misprint for "B." This is
implausible, because it is not easy to mistake an "H" for a "B" in
early eighteenth-century handwriting, and because the letter not
only occurs three times in quick succession but appears often in
Clio as the initial letter of "Hillarius," the name by which Fowke
and other members of Hill's circle referred to the addressee of
her memoir. The reasons why Hope is an improbable candidate
are that he was married by 30 March 1715, on which date he and
his wife had their daughter Mercy baptized; that his age of
twenty-seven (in 1720) seems inconsistent with the youthful
figure addressed in the poems;[46] that he was not "a Man of Bus-
iness" (1:264), if this means "One engaged in mercantile transac-
tions," since he is reported by his obituary to have been
"Attorney at Law and Deputy Remembrancer of the Court of Ex-
chequer" (2:165); and that his name does not fit the syllable pat-
tern suggested by the dashes in poems 12 and 16 (or indeed the
asterisks in the titles of poems 2 and 9, if their number matches
the letters they represent). Furthermore, although poem 24, "To
My Love. Wrote in Tears," foresees the ocean dividing the poet
from her lover, poem 23, "To Damon," published in the same
issue of the *Gazette*, names as threats to the relationship "Time,
new Friends, or cruel Interest" (31), and these are quite different
from the professional and domestic obligations that would have
caused Hope to return. Indeed, though Fowke says that her "Mr.
H——" was "bound to another" (*Clio*, p. 129), which could mean
either that he was engaged or already married, it seems unlikely
that she would have begun a relationship in which, she declares,
she "meant to have finished [her] Life," with a man who was not
only married but due shortly to return to Barbados.

THE OTHER FEMALE-AUTHORED LOVE POEMS

Guskin attributes to Martha Fowke not only the twenty-six
poems assigned to the anonymous lady but the fifteen other fe-

male-authored love poems in *Caribbeana*, along with the poem
of congratulation to William Gordon mentioned above. A third
part of her argument for linking all these poems to Fowke is
based on two of the fifteen not assigned to the anonymous lady.
The first, entitled "To Mr. -------- On His Having Resolved to Write
No More" (1:322–23), is one of the very few poems by women in
Caribbeana which is attributed, albeit by a pen-name, Clio. This
is the name under which Fowke wrote from about 1720 until 1726,
and Guskin suggests that the poem was addressed to Aaron Hill,
at some point before Fowke's relation with him reached the level
of intensity expressed by her memoir.[47] Hill was so enthusiastic
a writer that it is difficult to imagine him ever saying he would
give up his pen. However, he was involved in various ambitious
projects around 1720, he made an abortive attempt to return to
theatrical management in 1721–22,[48] and the style of the poem in
response to Clio's, printed immediately after it, is in keeping with
that of poems by him in Savage's *Miscellaneous Poems and
Translations* of 1726. Another possible candidate is John Dyer,
who also belonged to Hill's circle, and who trained as a painter.
The poem offers little evidence as to its date of composition, and
it is conceivable that it was written in the mid-1720s, when Dyer
was uncertain about his future career.[49]

A second poem not assigned to the anonymous lady that
Guskin attributes to Fowke is certainly connected with Dyer
(1:373–74, poem 39). Untitled, it begins: "To *Aberglasney*, lovely
place!," and, as Guskin points out, "Aberglasney was the family
home in Wales of John Dyer, poet and painter, who is clearly
identified by allusions to his poem 'Grongar Hill.' " Indeed,
Fowke and Dyer not only knew each other through their mutual
friend Hill, but Dyer painted her portrait, and the two exchanged
poems—some of which, along with an early version of "Grongar
Hill," were published in the Savage miscellany.[50] Guskin draws
attention to parallels between "To Aberglasney" and a poem by
Fowke in the Savage miscellany entitled "To Mr. Dyer": while
the one refers to "Household Cares" and "The *Hymenial* God,"
the other includes the lines: "I was, oh, hated Thought, a Woman
made; / For household Cares, and empty Trifles meant."[51] The
evidence that Fowke wrote "To Aberglasney" as well as the
poem assigned to Clio is therefore strong; and, in addition, "To
Aberglasney" contains a piece of verbal evidence suggesting a
link with the poems assigned to the anonymous lady. This con-

sists in the very rare word "Herdlings," which is recorded neither in the *OED* nor in the *English Dialect Dictionary*, and which occurs both in the poem addressed to Dyer (line 16) and in poem 23 by the anonymous lady, "To Damon" (line 10).

However, the dating of "To Aberglasney" raises a difficulty. It is unlikely that it could have been written before 1726, since its verse form is tetrameter couplets, echoing that of "Grongar Hill," to which it responds, and since Dyer seems not to have revised his poem in that form until that year.[52] Furthermore, Dyer is known to have returned to his home in the summer of 1726, and the poem's protests about "Household Cares" and "The *Hymenial* God" tally with the strong probability that at this time Fowke was obliged by her husband, Arnold Sansom, to withdraw from her life in the Hill circle which had exposed her to scandal.[53] If, as seems almost certain, the poem was written after 1721, it could not have been among the poems assigned to the anonymous lady, because these had been written by then. It therefore complicates the question of provenance, suggesting that the female-authored love poems in *Caribbeana* may have come from more than one source, and quite likely more than one writer.

Further evidence about dating also casts doubt on the identification of the anonymous lady with Martha Fowke. Among the three items from *Caribbeana* included by Roger Lonsdale in *Eighteenth-Century Women Poets* is the splendid riposte "On Being Charged with Writing Incorrectly" (poem 19). Though this is in key respects less a love poem than a poem about poetry, it was clearly written to a lover. The poet addresses a "Friend" (line 37), and she declares that she writes for her pleasure and his alone (37–40): "If I thy gentle Passions move, / 'Tis all I ask of Fame, or Love" (40–41). According to the correspondent who on Keimer's evidence supplied the poem, it was written when the poet "was not then above Nineteen" (1:314). If this claim is true, and if Fowke was the writer, then her birth year of 1689 means that the poem must have been completed by 1708. Guskin suggests that the poem may indeed have been written around that time, and that its presence among love poems written over ten years later "may well be explained by Fowke's pride in her precocious early writing."[54] This is an attractive way of explaining the discrepancy, but for several reasons it seems unlikely: the poem refers in lines 25–26 to John Dennis, whose notoriety as an

acerbic critic dates from his attack on Pope for the *Essay on
Criticism*; it seems to respond to the debate on the relation be-
tween nature and art in poetry to which Pope's poem gave new
life; and it is more sophisticated than the earliest poems as-
signed to Fowke, published like the *Essay on Criticism* in 1711.
It is possible that whoever reported the poet's age at the time
she wrote the poem did not tell the truth. But the poem's irrever-
ence and vivacity are very plausible attributes of a young writer,
and no work known to be by Fowke strikes quite the same note
of witty effrontery.

The Remaining Female-authored Love Poems in *Caribbeana*

The question of attribution is further complicated by the other
anonymous female-authored love poems in *Caribbeana*, not
least because Guskin has also suggested that these be assigned
to Fowke. As explained above, nine such poems appeared at ir-
regular intervals and over a much longer period than those as-
signed to the anonymous lady, while the remaining five were
published as a self-contained series in a single issue of the *Ga-
zette* in 1733.

There are plausible reasons for crediting Fowke with poem 39,
"To Aberglasney," discussed above. A less likely attribution,
poem 41, "A Pastoral Song," illustrates some of the dangers in-
herent in the task of identifying authorship. The poem could be
ascribed to Fowke on the grounds that, like much of her work,
it is a love poem, and that it draws on pastoral metaphors and
conventions, including such stock amatory vocabulary of the pe-
riod as the word "Flame." Other possible evidence is the pres-
ence of motifs which, as Guskin shows,[55] occur in work known to
be by Fowke: the theme of the poet's lost liberty (lines 5–6); the
word "tender" (30) and its cognates; and the use of physical and
sensual imagery, as when the poet describes her lover warming
her naked bosom with his own (17–20), and taking lambs to his
breast where only she has a right to rest herself (29–32). On the
other hand, it may be argued not only that amatory-pastoral
themes and language of this kind are entirely conventional, but
that, unlike the amatory verse acknowledged as Fowke's, this

poem does nothing to suggest that it goes beyond convention and refers to actual events of her life.[56] Further evidence against the attribution is that the verse form, tetrameter quatrains rhyming in couplets with a traditional refrain, is not elsewhere known to have been used by Fowke; neither does it occur in any of the poems assigned to the anonymous lady.

There are reasons for caution, then, in ascribing all the anonymous female-authored love poems in *Caribbeana* to the same author. Since verse-writing was a social accomplishment for the genteel, and since amatory poems of the period often use stock diction and conventions, especially from the pastoral tradition, it is not always easy, or possible, to distinguish the work of particular writers. The difficulty further increases with poets from a coterie such as Hill's—so that, for example, even the unusual word "herdlings" could have been borrowed from one writer by another. Thus the poems in *Caribbeana* not assigned to the anonymous lady could have been written by one or more other women. Nevertheless, it is not impossible that Fowke wrote some, even all, of the forty poems, including "A Pastoral Song." The remaining twelve unassigned poems offer some further evidence.

Part of this appears in the introductory comments to the five poems published in a single issue. Keimer's correspondent explains that these are juvenilia by a woman whose "riper and more study'd Performances" were admired, and who had only just been prevented from burning them, along with other verse she wished to destroy. He goes on to request that "the good-natured Critick will excuse any Incorrectness in the Poetry, when he considers that, being of the familiar Sort, it was never intended to be made publick" (1:151). Three points are consistent with the view that the poems are by Fowke: the writer was precocious; despite her youth, she not only wrote amatory verse but put together a sequence of poems, not intended for publication, to the same lover, as Fowke did for Hill; and her maturer work excited admiration. What seems unlikely is Guskin's suggestion that the poems refer to Fowke's relationship with the man who became her husband, Arnold Sansom,[57] since the marriage took place when she was at least thirty.

The remaining seven unassigned love poems offer few direct clues beyond their audacity of feeling and expression, and indeed five of them—poems 27, 29, 35, 36, and 40—are among those

printed without introduction or preliminary. However, the pas-
sion of these poems, and their lack of restraint, are a significant
common factor at a time when the moral and cultural codes gov-
erning female conduct and expression were tightening further.
The writer of poem 36 risks blasphemy by greeting Christmas
morning with exuberant tribute to her lover but not a word about
the birth of Christ; while the writer of poem 37 imagines herself
leaping from an upper window to the lover she is not allowed to
acknowledge, and paints a graphic picture of the potentially le-
thal consequences which alone hold her back. This kind of emo-
tional and imaginative daring is striking, and it is shared by the
poems assigned to the anonymous lady.

Two questions remain. First, there is Guskin's chief remaining
argument for attributing all the poems to Fowke—that of stylistic
and thematic parallels. Comparison of this kind has much to yield
in the case of the forty-one poems at issue, but, since the detailed
analysis it requires is not appropriate to an introduction, I re-
serve it for the afterword. Second, there is the wider problem of
why, if all the poems were by the same author, some were as-
signed to the so-called "amorous lady," one to Clio, a group of
five to a young woman who is not identified, others variously to
"a fair Lady" (1:26), "a Young Lady" (1:257, 1:300), "a young Lady
in *London*" (1:372), and "a Female Hand" (2:183), and the rest
left with no hint of the author's identity at all. These haphazard
pointers leave open a range of possible explanations.

At one end of the spectrum, it could be that Keimer and/or his
correspondent(s) told the truth. This would mean that the so-
called "amorous lady" wrote only the twenty-six poems assigned
to her, that Martha Fowke wrote the poem which appears under
her pen-name Clio, and that the remaining fourteen items were
written by one or more other women whose identities were not
known or could not be revealed. (*Caribbeana* does not say they
are not by the same woman; it does attribute five to a single au-
thor.) At the other end of the spectrum is the view argued by
Guskin: that the poems are all by the same woman, Martha
Fowke. But this leads to at least three further questions. One is
why all but one of the poems could not be attributed to Fowke—
or, at least, Clio. A second is why a single group of twenty-six
poems was assigned to a specific unnamed woman, and a group
of five poems, which in several ways are comparable, to another.

The first question is not difficult to answer, because all but one of the forty-one poems are potentially compromising. It is not just that they express feelings which women were not supposed to exhibit, even own. It is also that, taken together, they imply an author for whom contemporaries might have thought "amorous" too tame a word altogether. If all the poems are assigned to a single hand, and if they are given the autobiographical reading they invite, the writer must have been involved in passionate relationships with several different men. This might well have seemed too scandalous a scenario for readers of the *Barbados Gazette*, though it is no less than what *Clio* suggests, even while, writing for the eyes of her lover Hill, Fowke plays down her previous liaisons. Furthermore, Fowke did not write *Clio* for publication; and it is very unlikely that, whoever wrote the love poems in *Caribbeana*, any woman of the period would have wanted them in print, at least while they could still do damage. Conversely, the only one of these poems to appear under a name, albeit a pseudonym, contains nothing that might have compromised her (poem 38, "To Mr. -------- On His Having Resolved to Write No More"). Although the praise paid by this poem to its addressee is fulsome, it is in keeping with the tradition of complimentary verse amply displayed by Savage's miscellany, including some of the poems by Fowke.

The third question is more taxing. If all the poems are by the same woman, and if they found their way into print via the man to whom the majority were addressed, it is not easy to explain why she would have given her lover copies of passionate love poems she had previously addressed to other men. The contrast with *Clio* is sharp, for here Fowke not only sought to gloss over her past liaisons, but included only brief and bland verse she had written to her suitors. Poem 39, "To Aberglasney," presents a further problem. For reasons already discussed, this poem cannot have been written before 1726. If it is indeed by Fowke, the date is five or six years later than that of the poems by the anonymous lady. It seems highly implausible that, if Fowke was the anonymous lady, she would have given to the lover who had left her a later poem she wrote to another man. Instead, it is much more likely that the forty-one poems reprinted in this edition were supplied to Keimer by one or more other persons, in addition to the anonymous lady's addressee.

Finally, neither Fowke nor her husband could have been in a position to influence publication of the poems, if she wrote others beside the poem attributed to her by her pen name Clio. She had retired from the literary scene by the later 1720s, and Arnold Sansom died in January 1734, before most of the poems appeared. Fowke's brother Thomas, who was making a successful career in the army, would certainly have wanted to avoid family dishonor, an aim in which he apparently succeeded when he persuaded Fowke to marry Sansom early in the previous decade.[58] He was not, however, in Barbados; and it is difficult to imagine any influence he might have been able to exert extending there. It seems more likely, therefore, that identities were concealed at the insistence of the addressee and/or provider of the poems. If the addressee was married, he might not have wanted attention drawn to a past liaison; or he may have occupied a professional position which he wished to keep free from embarrassment. Unless or until his identity can be firmly established, there is scope only for speculation. No doubt the secrecy over names to some extent suited Keimer, who was able to heighten the interest of his readers with occasional teasing titbits of information.

There is also a possible aesthetic motivation for the manner in which the poems were printed. Keimer placed in a single issue the group of five poems which trace the vicissitudes of a love affair; and the poems by the anonymous lady have their own story to tell. The story has turning-points, as when the poet discovers that her lover writes poems too; and it has a sharply defined and moving finale when he leaves her in despair. Although the narrative is not continuous, and although the order of composition is often impossible to discern, part of the impact of the poems develops from the unfolding drama they outline. To present that drama is, in part, the purpose of this edition, which aims not only to introduce them to a much wider readership than they have enjoyed so far, but also to present them as a series which has its own integrity and coherence. What most justifies the edition is, however, the quality of the poems themselves—including some of those which were not assigned to the anonymous lady, such as "To Aberglasney" and the poem attributed to Clio. A case for the importance and distinction of the poems is set out in the Afterword.

A Letter to My Love

Poems by the Anonymous Lady

1. *On Reading Dr.* Donne's *Poems.*

In vain I to the Dead return,
To read how Lovers us'd to burn;
From *Cowley*'s melting Thoughts I rove,
To gentle *Waller*, fam'd for Love;
From them to *Lansdown*, I retire,   5
To *Congreve*, *Addison*, and *Prior.*
Their Art and Numbers I admire;
   Their different Beauties I confess;
   But oh! they wanted Tenderness.

Wit and Art their Numbers speak,   10
Fame they sought, but Love I seek:
Waller has a Softness too,
Something that I feel for you;
But my Heart cou'd teach his Lays
How to love; tho' not to praise: 15
Waller shou'd my Fondness bless,
   And, with weeping Eyes, confess
   My superior Tenderness.

Were my Passion to appear,
What Description would it bear?   20
All Conceits my Flame would wrong,
If it wou'd adorn my Song.
Be it the Business of my Thought,
To move thy Heart by Nature taught;
Art I scorn, forgive the Fault,   25
   And, with my fond Pen, confess
   Undissembled Tenderness.

Thy Eyes I will forbear to blame;
From Heaven itself my Passion came,
In every Atom of my Frame;   30
My Hands, my Feet, my Soul agree,
And every Nerve in loving thee.
My trembling Fingers write the Lines,
Which the Neighbouring Soul divines;

My Heart, with Beatings too, confess,   35
With the rest, its Tenderness.

Didst thou not the Fondling hear,
Courting tenderly thy Ear;
As you lean'd upon my Breast,
It my very Soul express'd.   40
As my Eyes were ranging o'er
All the Beauties I adore,
With a Joy unknown before;
   Did not Silence self confess,
   Then, a World of Tenderness?   45

Say, has any Bosom shown
Half my Love?—Oh! not thy own.
Show my Eyes, or faithful Heart,
Such a Passion, free from Art:
Let my Soul be open laid,   50
In Absence all my Thoughts survey'd,
Every Wish that it has made;
  Then with Love itself confess
   My unbounded Tenderness.

2. *To* * * * * * * * *

Believe me; but my Actions speak
   Thy Merit and my Truth;
Here all Expressions are too weak,
   My dear engaging Youth.

Words faintly would my Love define,   5
   If Words thou did'st approve;
My Eyes, my Arms, my Soul are thine,
   And all reveal my Love.

There is no Atom in this Frame
   That does not talk to thee,   10
And sigh and tremble at thy Name,
   And plead for Love, and me.

Oh! listen to my beating Heart,
   When thy dear Head reclines;
But, if it fail to speak its Part,   15
   Attend my melting Lines.

With tender Passion they are fraught,
   Nor dread the Critick's Ear,
While gentle *Cupid* tunes my Thought,
   And is the Poet here.   20

3. To the SAME.

Lost to my longing Arms and Eyes,
My Heart to this soft Method flies;
The only One that has a Pow'r
From me to give thee one soft Hour:
Not all the Artful of thy Kind   5
Can, like this Paper, sooth my Mind;
Such Pow'r thy much lov'd Name can give
To this, that, while I write, *I live.*
Oh! so extravagant's my Flame,
I kiss each Letter of thy Name: 10
My Lips do oft too rudely press
The Lines with cruel Tenderness.
Love to my Soul ungentle grows;
Nor Bounds, nor Moderation knows:
A Thousand foolish Things I do;   15
Myself forgetting, while I think on you;
My Life, my Soul, my Pleasure and Employ;
The Business of my Thought, my lovely Boy;
My tender Master who has taught me more,
In one short Year, than Ages did before.   20

4. *To the SAME. A PASTORAL.*

With what unwearied Fondness I admire,
Tell to my gentle Love, my gentle Lyre:
The Words of *Antony* how I approve;
"One Day past by, and nothing saw but Love;
"Another Day, till Months and Years were tir'd,   5

"With looking on, our Passions unexpir'd.
Near thee for ever I could pass the Hours,
But Friends or Business half the Time devours;
A very few are left to Love and me;
Oh! wer't thou all my own, from Business free,   10
Enough Employment wou'd my Fondness find,
A thousand Methods to amuse thy Mind.
To some sweet Grotto I'd my Dearest guide,
Where the Sun shou'd not see me by thy Side;
My Head shou'd on thy dear lov'd Bosom lean,   15
And Love be by, to bless the tender Scene.
When tir'd with hearing my unweary'd Flame,
I then would woo thee in some other Name.
Waller himself my Advocate should be,
Reading his Passion, gazing oft on thee.   20
Oh! with what Pride I should thy Bosom dress,
Kissing the Flowers with jealous Tenderness;
The tuneful Linnets to thy Hand I'll bring,
And teach them on thy very Breast to sing;
My Favourite Dog shall at thy Feet attend,   25
If e'er I go, my Charmer to defend;
Safe may'st thou slumber, if the grateful Brute,
Who loves thee well, but watches at thy Foot.
What shall I say to shew I love indeed?
Accept my Darling Crook, my tuneful Reed;   30
My Books, and all the Sonnets you approve;
Oh! read them well; for they express my Love;
Nor Tongue, nor Eyes, nor Numbers can explain
My Deathless Passion, for my lovely Swain.

5. *Occasioned by his Illness.*

While for thy precious Life I fear,
From every Pore descends a Tear;
My Soul and Body feels, for thee,
An Universal Agony:
No Wonder if my Fears are more,   5
Who loves as none e'er lov'd before;
The little Floods will not suffice,
That Nature gives the weeping Eyes;

O'er all my Limbs a deathly Dew;
Others may mourn, but I shall die with you. 10
With thine, behold my Face grow pale,
My Speech all broken, and my Spirits fail.
My Eyes are on thy Features fix'd;
My Looks with Death and Sorrow mixt.
Something beyond ev'n Death, I find, 15
That hurts not the impassive Mind:
But here my very Soul is press'd,
And languishes within my Breast:
My trembling Hands the Pen refuse,
And Sorrow has undone my Muse. 20
Oh! Can I ever live to see
That Bosom press'd so oft by me,
Panting and lost for Want of Breath,
And those dear Eyes shut up in Death?
Distracting Thought! for thee I'll drain 25
My own Heart's Blood, and every Vein,
To make thy Channels flow again.
But if thy Soul will force its Way;
If Tears nor Groans will bribe its Stay,
Our Lips in the last Gasp shall join, 30
I'll catch thy Soul and give thee mine:
Till then, I'll near thy Bed attend,
My Eyes shall watch, my Knees shall bend;
The Stars my Midnight Hours shall see,
The Stars shall learn to watch of me: 35
Thy Cordials I will give with Care,
But, if a Tear shou'd mingle there,
Forgive my Fondness,———know that she,
Who weeps, as soon wou'd die for thee.
If thy Pulse move too slow a Pace, 40
My Sighs shall wing them in their Race;
Or, if too fast, my Tears shall chide
Thy beating Veins, and check the Tide.

6. *His PICTURE.*

Gentle Love, to paint my Lover,
  Let thy Pencil be thy Dart;

Every killing Grace discover,
    That is glowing in my Heart.

Be his lovely Eyes defining,   5
    But 'tis fatal to approach,
Where a thousand Charms are shining;
    I, alas! have gaz'd too much.

Be thy Pencil now descending,
    But descend with tender Care;   10
Lest the new-born Smiles offending,
    That are ever springing there.

Gently glide o'er every Feature
    With bewitching Softness form'd;
In his Composition, Nature   15
    Was by *Love* and *Bacchus* warm'd.

Touch his Lips design'd for Pressing,
    Where thy own fond Mother lies;
Everlasting Love expressing,
    From his Mouth, and from his Eyes.   20

Now his Shape and Air surveying,
    How I chide my artless Song!
I my Fondness am betraying,
    But have done his Beauties wrong.

Oh! how ill I am performing,   25
    Tho' assisted by thy Dart;
Damon's Picture is more charming,
    It has painted in my Heart.

7. *Written on one of his Letters.*

To thee, dear Letter, I impart
All the Anguish of my Heart.
Oh! compose its racking Care,
Pour thy healing Softness there;
Since a thousand cruel Forms   5

Keep thy Master from my Arms;
Thou a while his Place supply,
To my trembling Bosom lie;
Often whisper his dear Name,
To Advantage dress his Flame;   10
That no Jealousy may dare,
To alarm me with a Care;
Breathe his Sighings such a Way,
That I to my Soul may say,
'He, my Love, my Life, is here,   15
'What beside cou'd charm my Ear? }
'What beside cou'd be so dear?
If I to a Slumber fall,
Thou shalt waken at my Call;
Ev'ry soft inchanting Line   20
Shall, in Spight of Midnight, shine;
Gentle Love shall smiling see
All my Tenderness to thee;
And shall bless the happy Hour,
When she gave thee so much Pow'r.   25

8. *On a FAN presented.*

Not the *Trojan* triumph'd more,
When the Golden Fleece he bore;
My Hand, with equal Pleasure, takes
The Gift thy tender Friendship makes;
The Way of giving lends it Charms,   5
And so endears it to my Arms.
This soft Machine, for Air design'd,
At every Furl leaves Flames behind.
Of Magick Wood the Poet sings;
Of sighing Plants, and plaintive Springs: 10
This Ivory boasts an equal Force;
Can raise, and can prolong Discourse;
And, when with Modish Anger flung,
It drowns the Jarring of the Tongue.
For many Wonders it is worn;   15
Or to shew Tenderness, or Scorn;
To give Denial to the Fool;

To curb the Bold, inspire the Cool.
But oh! whene'er it gives a Sign,
To any wishing Eye but thine,   20
May all the Silver Studs (avert
That Omen!) from each other, part:
May the dear Sticks together jar,
Lie wounded, and not find *Colemar*.
May it its every Beauty lose,   25
And its inchanting Flap refuse.

9. *To Mr.* * * * * * *

Oh! what retains thee now, what new Design,
With-holds thy loit'ring Heart from meeting mine?
What dull Excuses can thy Slowness frame,
To my poor longing Arms and boundless Flame?
My wishing Senses all demand their Right,   5
My trembling Bosom, and my aching Sight;
My Eyes are dying to behold thy Face,
And tir'd with searching thee in every Place,
Whilst my Soul sighs to Death, for thy Embrace.
Does not the Winds its ardent Sighings bear?   10
Is not thy Breast struck with a stranger Air?
Oh! let my tender Wishes enter there.
Why hast thou done my fond Expectance Wrong,
And held me from my Paradise so long?
My Life, my Love, my Happiness restore;   15
Not dying Saints wish for their Heaven more.

10. *The APPEAL.*

Let Love be Judge between us two,
    Who best observes his Laws;
But he's a Youth as well as you,
    And partial to your Cause.

Where shall my luckless Heart pretend,   5
    Justice or Truth to find;
Since you no longer are my Friend,
    And Love is brib'd and blind?

But let him say, if e'er his Dart
   A softer Bosom knew;   10
If e'er it pierc'd a kinder Heart,
   Than this which sighs for you.

Let bright *Apollo* hold the Scales,
   He'll do our Passions Right;
Shew us whose Tenderness prevails,   15
   And which is much too light.

But oh! I fear thy giddy Youth
   My fatal Search will find,
Fly up, and leave my heavy Truth
   Sunk on the Ground behind.   20

For, if it was repleat before,
   Alas! what now wil't prove?
With Sighs and Tears it will run o'er,
   If they have Weight in Love.

Hold up thy Hand, oh! much-lov'd Swain,   25
   While the poor Plainant pleads;
And know, while I thy Heart arraign,
   My own with Sorrow bleeds.

11. *The COMPLAINT.*

How sadly heavy has this Day,
Oh! my sweet Angel! crept away?
The Hours have, sure, forgot to move;
Alas! the Hours were ne'er in Love.
For it is by the Poets told,   5
That Time (oh! happy Man!) is old;
He feels not my incessant Pains,
Nor does he hear my dying Strains.
Yet, by thy silver shining Hair,
Thy Heart has known a Lover's Care.   10
What else could make thee grey or old,
But the lov'd Object's being cold?
If so, oh! let thy Care be shown;

Pity the Torments thou hast known:
And, when my dearest Love and I   15
Are sat together, do not fly;
Oh! then thy ebbing Sands delay,
Make every Hour a Summer's Day.

12. *The ABSENT.*

I.

I gave thy Merit up my Heart,
  Uncounsel'd by the Wise;
I ask'd no low Advice of Art,
  But of thy lovely Eyes,
Which saw my Soul in every Part,   5
  And all its Wishes rise.

II.

My leaping Vein, my trembling Tongue,
  The soft Disease explain;
My Lips, where falt'ring Accents hung,
  And strove to speak in vain;   10
My Lyre, which once my Freedom sung,
  Now groans beneath my Chain.

III.

To one lov'd Object still confin'd,
  To sigh my deathless Flame;
For that neglecting all Mankind,   15
  My Interest and my Fame;
To every other Theme unkind,
  But lovely *Damon*'s Name.

IV.

The Learned of their Friends enquire,
  While I all absent sit;   20
Is this the Muse the Men admire,
  And whilom call'd a *Wit?*

Has the *South-Sea* undone her Lyre?
 But———heeds not yet.

V.

Dead to the Company, my Eyes   25
 Are fix'd upon the Ground;
Or else perchance in Tears they rise,
 The Laughter passes round;
No social Friend a Tear applies,
 Or Counsel to my Wound.   30

VI.

Oh! see the Mischiefs thou hast wrought,
 How will thy Heart attone,
For the Distraction of my Thought,
 Employ'd on thee alone?
Oh! gentle *Damon*, hide the Fault,   35
 With greater of thy own.

13. *SONG.*

While my Eyes are fondly speaking,
 They with killing Anguish see,
Thine some newer Face is seeking,
 Careless of my Griefs, and me.

While my Soul itself expressing,   5
 How can yours unmindful be?
With your faithless Looks addressing,
 Careless of my Griefs, and me.

Oh! what Torments do I suffer,
 While our Hearts so ill agree!   10
Grow a more obsequious Lover,
 Or no longer think of me.

In the World I may discover
 Something that may charm like thee,
Or I'll live without a Lover;   15
 If not thine, I will be free.

Hopes and Fears are too oppressing
  For my tender Breast, I see;
Give me back, my Stars! the Blessing
  Of my banish'd Liberty.   20

Or else form some gentle Creature,
  That may with my Soul agree;
That will prove as hard to Nature,
  As a Change will be to me.

14. *The PROTESTATION.*

I've Love enough to brilliant every Line,
To dress my Flame, and make my Numbers fine;
But when I think their Beauties will expire,
E're thy dear Eyes have Leisure to admire;
To cruel Prudence still an Off'ring made,   5
My Soul is damp'd, and its Ideas fade.
The dying *Sappho* lovely *Phaon* sung;
No Fetters bound her Fancy or her Tongue;
By Love to Immortality she soar'd,
Fame crown'd her Temples, while her Heart ador'd.   10
To equal Glory I perchance cou'd raise
Thy Mistress too, had she a Right to Praise;
But from the only Object I'm confin'd,
That can give Love or Glory to my Mind.
See how my Genius and my Hopes are crost,   15
Oh! give me Love for all that I have lost.
For Fame, Repose, and God-like Liberty,
For all that I have been, or I might be,
Oh! give me Love, and Love bestow me thee.

15. *To DAMON.*

Go, faithful Paper, to my Love impart
All the soft Things his Eyes have taught my Heart;
Learn from my Cheeks a paler Look to wear,
And copy every Tear that's streaming there;
Catch of my Sighs the melancholy Tone;   5
And imitate the Midnight dying Groan.

To his dear Soul my Agonies impart,
The everlasting Beatings of my Heart:
Oh! let my Sorrow an Adviser be;
For Grief itself might learn to look of me: 10
Tremble, as I do now, when you complain,
And say, *Thus shook her Soul at every Strain.*
Thus sunk her Voice, all faint her Accents grew;
But her last parting Breath was blessing you.
Then will he fold thee to his lovely Breast, 15
Where *Venus'* Doves, or *Venus'* self might rest.
The Spring's united Sweetness you will find,
The Damask Rose, and new-born Vi'let join'd;
The *Tuby-Rose, Carnation*, and *John-quill*;
Fraught with new Sweets, from every Pore distil. 20
But why do I his fragrant Bosom Wrong,
With Similes that only grace my Song?
For, oh! its matchless Sweetness is above
All Things on Earth, form'd by the God of Love,
Who has adorn'd him with his Mother's Charms; 25
And to her killing Eyes has join'd his Arms.
   Oh! who can say which Sense he pleases most?
     He has peculiar Art to touch them all;
    Not Virtue's self its Icy Pow'r can boast;
      The Soul and Body hastens to his Call. 30
Superior Magick to his Arms convey'd,
Than * *His* who warm'd to Life the jolly Maid;
He has a Godlike Power to create;
He made me love, ah, cou'd he make me hate!
I then no soft Ambassador shou'd need; 35
Nor would I trouble thee, soft Friend, to plead.
I tremble, lest the Paper, I've convey'd,
Itself be warm'd into some happy Maid;
Cou'd the cold Statue kindle into Fire?
What wilt thou do, who burns with my Desire! 40

* *Pygmalion.*

16. *To the SAME.*

While to thy dear lov'd Arms I press,
   And tremble o'er thy Breast;

I love thee to such kind Excess,
    That I but half am blest.

The Fear of losing thee pursues   5
    My fond foreboding Heart;
My present Happiness I lose,
    With dreading once to part.

In vain Philosophy appears,
    To reason me to Rest,   10
And stop the gushing Tide of Tears,
    I pour upon thy Breast.

In vain gay Youth its Flattery brings
    Of Fortune and Address:
It talks a thousand idle Things;   15
    But, oh! without Success.

It tells what Lovers wait my Call,
    And for my Favour press;
But they, alas! are tasteless all
    To ———'s Tenderness.   20

The God of Verse himself appears,
    And promises my Name
Shall brightly shine in future Years;
    But what is Life, or Fame?

Nor Life, nor Fame, my Bosom chears,   25
    They have no longer Charms;
Ye Powers, that promise smiling Years,
    Give them in *Damon*'s Arms!

17. *To the SAME*.

Let the God of Passion hear me,
It is Heaven to be near thee,
By thy lovely Eyes I swear,
And the Train of *Cupids* there;
I wou'd not thy Arms resign,   5

If a Monarch sigh'd for mine.
Thou wer't for my Wishes made,
To inchant me, to perswade;
While I fondly gaze upon thee,
While my Soul is doating on thee,   10
To my Lips it eager flies,
Or to my desiring Eyes.
On my Breast it will not stay,
By its Master charm'd away;
If thou lik'st, my Soul, then prithee   15
Keep the Fondling ever with thee;
For I have no Use for one,
When my dearer Soul is gone;
Then a kind of Corps I seem,
And not *live*, but only *dream*.   20
In thy Absence I am dead,
Folded Arms and drooping Head:
If a Lover talks to me;
Still I answer him with thee;
Hear, he cries, *my raging Flame*,   25
Unawares, I sigh *thy Name*;
Oh! what Hope for any other,
Wheresoe'er thou art a Lover?
By thy Tenderness ingross'd,
None can land upon that Coast.   30
To some other Island bear
Common Sighs of empty Air;
Damon's Empire in my Heart
Interest will not shock, nor Art.

18. *To the SAME*.

Tho', blind with Love, I well perceive
   Thy Tenderness decline;
Think not my Passion long can live,
   Without the Warmth of thine.

From thy dear Eyes my Flames I took,   5
   They taught them first to shine;
How does the languid *Cynthia* look,
   Till *Phoebus* makes her fine?

Nor Heat, nor Beauty of her own,
   She borrows all her Light;   10
And it is from thy Beams alone,
   I either love, or write.

Thy Fondness is the Fountain, where
   My Fondness first begun;
If thou art cold, mine stagnates there;   15
   And will no longer run.

Wonder not, if you see my Eyes
   To the sad Earth decline;
The Strings that let them fall, or rise,
   Nature entrusts to thine.   20

What Pity 'tis my Soul shou'd be
   So much within thy Pow'r;
By Heaven's! I long for Liberty,
   And only for an Hour.

From Heart to Heart my Sighs shou'd beat,   25
   Till they a Haven found,
Where Ship-wreck'd Fondness might retreat,
   And every Wish be crown'd.

19. *On being charged with Writing incorrectly.*

I'm incorrect, the Learned say,
That *I write well, but not their Way.*
For this to every Star I bend;
From their dull Method Heaven defend;
Who labour up the Hill of Fame,   5
And pant and struggle for a Name;
My freeborn Thoughts I'll not confine,
Tho' all *Parnassus* could be mine.
No, let my Genius have its Way,
My Genius I will still obey;   10
Nor, with their stupid Rules, controul
The sacred Pulse that beats within my Soul.
I, from my very Heart, despise

These mighty dull, these mighty wise,
Who were the Slaves of *Busby*'s Nod,   15
And learn'd their Methods from his Rod.
Shall bright *Apollo* drudge at School,
And whimper till he grows a Fool?
Apollo, to the Learned coy,
In Nouns and Verbs finds little Joy;   20
The tuneful Sisters still he leads
To Silver Streams and flow'ry Meads;
He glories in an artless Breast,
And loves the Goddess Nature best.
Let *Dennis* hunt me with his Spite,   25
Let me read *Dennis* every Night,
Or any Punishment sustain,
To 'scape the Labour of the Brain.
Let the Dull think, or let 'em mend
The trifling Errors they pretend;   30
Writing's my Pleasure, which my Muse
Wou'd not for all their Glory lose:
With Transport I the Pen employ,
And every Line reveals my Joy:
No Pangs of Thought I undergo,   35
My Words descend, my Numbers flow;
Tho' disallow'd, my Friend, I'd swear,
I wou'd not think, I wou'd not care,
If I a Pleasure can impart,
Or to my own, or thy dear Heart;   40
If I thy gentle Passions move;
'Tis all I ask of Fame, or Love.
This to the very Learned say;
If they are angry,————why they may;
I, from my very Soul, despise   45
These mighty dull, these mighty wise.

20. Untitled

To my gentle Damon *haste;*
Pour my Soul into his Breast,
Where I wish myself to rest.

To my Breast thy Verse applying,
   Jealousy is heard no more;
Were I on the Point of dying,
   It would every Pulse restore.
Now I am with Transport crying,   5
   As I did with Pain before.

While thy Soul itself expressing
   In so dear, so sweet a Key;
Mine, an equal Flame confessing,
   Sounds in every Line to thee;   10
Oh my everlasting Blessing,
   Form'd by Love himself for me!

While I to thy Arms am pressing,
   All the World is lost to me:
If *Apollo* were addressing,   15
   I would turn into a *Tree*,
And be cold to his Caressing,
   Fondly thus to gaze on thee.

If he with his Stars descended,
   And would give them all to me;   20
Wer't thou poor and unbefriended,
   I would yield them all for thee;
With such Truths the Love's attended,
   Which now fills my Breast for thee.

I, no Tenderness disguising,   25
   Pour out every Thought to thee;
Every little Art despising,
   Which with meaner Hearts agree;
Take my Soul, as it is rising,
   Flowing in my Verse to Thee.   30

If with Truth I can retain thee,
   Oh how happy I shall be!
Let these Arms for ever chain thee;
   Never wishing to be free;
If their eager Pressings pain thee,   35
   Pay back all the Wrongs on me.

Be with Tenderness surveying,
   Think how great my Love must be;
My Heart, for Numbers never staying,
   Flies almost in Prose to thee;   40
And the God of Love, obeying,
   Thinks not of my Fame, nor me.

21. A Letter to my Love.——All alone, past 12, in the Dumps.

Absent from all that cou'd inspire
My Numbers, or my Soul, with Fire.

Oh! weep with me, the changing Scene,
Torn from thy Arms; devour'd with Spleen;
Instead of those dear Eyes, I look
Upon the Fire, or else a Book:
But Oh how dull must either be   5
To Eyes that have been studying thee!
Unless the Poet does express
Something that strikes my Tenderness,
I throw the Leaves neglected by,
And in my Chair supinely lie;   10
Or to the Pen and Ink I haste,
And there a World of Paper waste.
All I can write, tho' Love is here,
Does much unlike my Soul appear.
Angry, the scrawling Side I turn,   15
I write and blot, and write and burn;
Then to the Bottle I repair,
The Poets tell us Ease is there:
But I thy absent Hand repine,
Whose Sweetness us'd to *zest* the Wine;   20
Wine in this sullen Moment fails;
I burn my Pen, I bite my Nails,
Rail at my Stars, nay, I accuse
Even my Lover, and my Muse.
Why did he let me go, I cry,   25
——And, now I think on't, tell me why?
You might have kind Excuses made

To one so willing to ha' staid:
The Night was rainy, and the Wind
To all thy softest Wishes kind.   30
For thee and Love methought it blew, ⎤
As if my parting Pains it knew,   ⎬
As if it was a Lover too.   ⎦
I'm safely shaded from its Pow'r;
But I regard its Rage no more: 35
Now let it tempest as it please,
Or move the Groves, or fright the Seas;
It cannot now alarm my Rest,
Unless it reach thy dearer Breast.
Oh! hasten to me; let my Arms   40
Protect thee from the wintry Storms.
I tremble lest the Cold should dare
To pierce thee———let my Image, there,
Defend it, if it has a Charm,
From these and every other Harm.   45
I want thy Bosom to repose
My beating Heart, oppress'd with Woes;
I want thy Voice my Soul to chear,
Thy Voice is Musick to my Ear;
I want thy dear lov'd Hand to press   50
My Neck, with silent Tenderness;
I want thy Eyes to make me bright,
And charm this sullen Hour of Night.
This Hour, when pallid Ghosts appear,
Oh! cou'd it bring thy Shadow here;   55
I every Substance wou'd resign,
To clasp thy Aerial Breast to mine;
Or if, my Love, that could not be,
I would turn Air to mix with thee.

22. *Occasion'd by some Lines of his.*

1.

While you so sweetly sing your Flame,
   My list'ning Soul admires;
But jealous of its dying Fame,
   While thine so high aspires.

Where has thy Genius slept so long?   5
Oh! thou hast done my Fondness wrong!

2.

Coud'st thou a softer Subject chose,
    Than Passion so refin'd;
It wou'd have tun'd ungentle Prose,
    And every Letter join'd.   10
The Words would, like our Bosoms, meet,
    And, as our Arms, the downy Feet.

3.

Behold, great God of soft Desire,
    My Love's harmonious Strain;
I bless thy Power that aids his Lyre,   15
    So gently to complain;
In all the Arts of Verse unknown,
He trusted to thy Dart alone.

4.

Let others stupid Methods seek,
    And to *Parnassus* toil,   20
By *Latin* and loud sounding *Greek*,
    And plough the rugged Soil;
Love, in one Hour, informs them more
Than *Busby* cou'd in Years before.

5.

Oh! with thy gentle Master stay,   25
    Who has such Wonders wrought;
Nor from these Arms depart away,
    Where first thy Soul was taught;
My Lips shall pay thee every Line,
And all *Parnassus* shall be thine.   30

6.

The labouring Poets, distanc'd now
    By thy superior Race,

Shall rave and pant, and wonder how
   You reach'd, so soon, the Place.
They for thy Master will enquire,   35
Say, *'Twas a Mistress tun'd thy Lyre.*

7.

Bid 'em unlearn the odious Rules,
   That keep them back so long;
The heavy Luggage of the Schools,
   Which does their Fancy wrong.   40
Oh! bid them read thy artless Lines,
Where Love, and lovely Nature, shines.

8.

Trust me, my most belov'd and dear,
   Thy Heart will Credit find;
The Musick of it enters here,   45
   And softens all my Mind:
Now every Passion, to thy Lays,
A new and sweet Obedience pays.

9.

So lavish Nature was before
   To thy engaging Face,   50
She had but this one Beauty more,
   This one resistless Grace;
With this the Victory is whole,
And I deliver up my Soul.

Sign'd and Seal'd in the Presence of the God of Love *and the* Muses.

23. *To* DAMON.

In vain, oh! much in vain, for Rest I seek;
My Lips miss thine, my Cheek thy softer Cheek:
From Side to Side, the live-long Night I move,
No longer press'd by the dear Arms I love:

No longer I thy trembling Accents hear,   ⎤   5
Soft as an Angel's melting in my Ear,   ⎬
My Life, my Angel, my enchanting Dear. ⎦
Oh what a Harmony thy Voice affords,
When tun'd by Love to those endearing Words!
Softer than Reeds that do the Herdlings call,   10
Or Summer-Winds, or Waters when they fall.
Oh my Delight! when thy dear Form was made,
The Gods of Love and Musick lent their Aid;
The gentle Atoms in such Order fell,
That Nature smiling said, *The Piece is well.*   15
A Thousand *Cupids*, with peculiar Grace,
Command the Muscles of thy pleasing Face.
How oft my Heart has bless'd their little Toil,
And leap'd within my Breast at ev'ry Smile;
Various Attractions call my Muse to praise,   20
My Verse, my Wishes charm'd a Thousand Ways:
Shall I the Beauties of thy Soul commend,
Which warms the Form I love, and is my Friend?
'Tis that, my lovely Youth, inspires thy Charms,
Sits on thy Lips, and strains me to thy Arms: 25
A Thousand Blessings all its Wishes wait,
Sweeten its Hours, and Death be wondrous late:
E're that arrives, Oh! may I right divine!
May I be dead, if I'm no longer thine;
If thou, my Soul, art parted from my Breast,   30
By Time, new Friends, or cruel Interest;
The killing Thought my ready Tears demands,
Stabs my poor Heart, and sinks my trembling Hands.
Oh! come, my dearest Life, and give me Rest,
My Arms are tir'd with folding on my Breast: 35
My weeping Eyes do for thy Features long;
My Hearing, for the Musick of thy Tongue.
Oh! ev'ry Sense will die without thee soon,
And Soul and Body both be out of Tune.

24. *To my* LOVE. *Wrote in Tears.*

Dearest Creature of thy Kind,
All that can transport my Mind;

While I hold thee to my Breast,
Ev'ry Wish but *one* is blest;
That some sad Hour (O Heav'n remove   5
It far!) must take me from my Love.
Seas must our longing Arms divide,
The Winds oppose, and raging Tide;
Then shall I wish *Leander*'s Arms,
To force the Waves, and meet thy Charms,   10
Then shall I curse my feeble Kind,
And wish my Body all o'er Mind.
Oh! wilt thou then, far from my Sight,
Forget to love, forbear to write?
Or wilt thou sigh, when thou art told   15
———, thy once belov'd, is cold.
Thy Absence gave the mortal Blow;
She ceas'd to live, she lov'd thee so.
When Fate or Chance directs thy Way
To *England*, visit my sad Clay.   20
Oh! as you kneel before my Shrine,
Wonder not if thy Sighs I join;
My Bosom, us'd to mourn for thee,
Will to thy Voice an Eccho be.

25. *To my* LOVE.

1.

When in my fond Embraces fast confin'd,
    My trembling Arms my Agonies express'd,
No Tear in sad Society was join'd,
    To chear me pale and speechless on thy Breast;
Scarce had I Life from thy dear Sight to part,   5
So fix'd my Eyes; so full my breaking Heart.

2.

Fain would my Lips have sigh'd, *Adieu, Adieu!*
    But rising Sorrow would not give them Leave;
My Words, like Traitors, they forsook me too;
    My Sighs themselves had scarcely Pow'r to heave;   10

My Arms alone with Grasping could impart
The Agony that fill'd my breaking Heart.

3.

As I a thousand thousand Times embrac'd,
　Hoping by every one to make thee kind;
In vain my weeping Eyes thy Features trac'd   15
　(And Features speak the Passions of the Mind)
Still wert thou unconcern'd; nor didst impart
One Sigh of thine, to those that swell'd my Heart.

4.

While I was griev'd to such a kind Excess;
　Oh! how untimely must thy Prudence be,   20
To bid me *meet, with artful Tenderness,*
　The Arms that were no Friends to Love or thee.
Beware how you instruct me in that Part,
Lest I give him the true, and thee the faithless Heart.

5.

Bid the rude North be gentle to the Spring,   25
　Or kiss the new-born Flowers with tender Care;
To Reconcilements all Aversions bring;
　But oh! to me thy dull Advice forbear;
No faithless Maxims to my Breast impart,
To change the Nature of my breaking Heart.   30

26. *To the Same.*

Time's Wings are lost now thy dear Eyes are gone,
Droops with my Cares and heavily creeps on;
'Tis thy Return that only can impart
A Spring to them or to my breaking Heart.
Absence and Love! too much at once to bear; ⎫   5
Come soon, or they will waste thy Empire there; ⎬
The Lamp of Life will sink with killing Care! ⎭
Oh! bring thy Bosom to support my Head,
And catch my Soul e're it too far is fled;

Let not thy Friends another Hour entreat,   10
Lest ———'s Corps be laid beneath thy Feet,
Oh! will it pain thy Eyes to see this Face,
Where once the Muses spread a little Grace;
Where thou and Love in gentle Triumph shone,
Her Days, her Life, her Love for ever gone;   15
When thy soft Hand shall touch her chilly Breast,
Where the soft God and thou wert wont to rest;
When it no more thy gentle Touch shall meet,
No more the Heart within with Transport beat.
Will thy Hand drop the Glass with sad Surprise?   20
Wilt thou kneel down, and kiss my clos'd up Eyes?
———Thy Friends will of thy Tenderness complain,
And Wine and Wit will raise a Laugh again.

Other Female-Authored
Anonymous Love Poems

27. *To———*

Love, deathless Love, is the most noble Sign
That Heav'n has stamp'd, to shew the Soul divine:
If there's a Soul that loves beyond the rest,
The Angels guard it, and approve it best.
Then mine, this Way, will merit all their Care,   5
For I love more than any Angel there:
More Tenderness for thy dear Breast I find,
Than for their Charge, those Guardians of Mankind.

28. *Written at Midnight.*

How tedious the long wintry Night appears,
To unclos'd Eyes, which pass it all in Tears!
Or if they close, how dreadful is the Dream!
Some raging Lion, or some rapid Stream!
My Spirits sunk, all pale and out of Breath,   5
Toiling with this imaginary Death;
The melancholy Shadows of the Day,
Does on my Soul in mournful Slumbers stay;
For oh! my Griefs are of so sad a Kind,
They pierce my Sense, and even kill my Mind;   10
My Dreams are with a thousand Dangers fraught,
The mournful Pictures of my waking Thought;
My Passions stagger underneath the Blow,
And my Heart-breaking Strings refuse to go:
Shou'd Fate grow kind, and my lost Love restore,   15
It cou'd leap up to meet his Eyes no more.
Why nam'st thou Love, the Tyrant of thy Breast,
That blights thy Bays, and murders all thy Rest?
The fatal Sound is Poison to my Frame,
Wakes all my Wounds, and fewels every Flame.   20
Oh, how I burn, for a cold Icy Breast,
Which, like a God, is by my Love addrest,
With Sighs and Tears, and Groans, and broken Rest!
Oh! witness for me, ev'ry doubled Hour,
To my Soul's Anguish, and my Passion's Pow'r.   25
A thousand Times, and more, I change my Side;

Restless I lie, and my poor Pillow chide;
Like a pale Ghost, I pass the heavy Night,
Traverse the Room out, watch the dying Light.
Alas! behold, the weary Taper fades,   30
And gives my Sorrow up to gloomy Shades;
To Thoughts, to mournful Thoughts, that darker are,
Than the veil'd Midnight Skies, without a Star.
Be still, ye Winds, my louder Sighs attend,
And you, fair Stream, to which my Tears descend,   35
The Sun will not this many an Hour arise,
The happy Sun in *Thetis'* Bosom lies;
He needs ye not; alas! my Griefs alone
Are waking now, or Souls that Grief have known.
This is the Hour that troubled Spirits rove,   40
Sacred to melancholy hopeless Love.
All Things but Death, and Deathless Sorrow, rest,
Such as alarm my ever waking Breast.
Oh, could this Hand some friendly Weapon find,
To let out Life, and free my Captive Mind!   45
What holds it back? alas! Is there a Fear
I cou'd be more undone than I am here?
In some new World I long my Fate to try;
Vouchsafe, then, Heav'ns! to let your Mortal die.
Prometheus, fasten'd to the Rock, complains,   50
Whilst the rag'd Vulture drinks his bleeding Veins;
Thus Love and Sorrow every Joy devours,
Feeds on my Soul, and all my tender Hours.

29. To * * * * * * *

Whene'er I leave thee, my unwilling Mind
Stays, like a weary Traveller, behind;
Or like some wretched Ghost whom Death has prest,
E're its appointed Hour, to leave the Breast;
It wanders back again, and hovers o'er   5
The Place where all its Treasure lay before.
I strive to bear thy Absence, but in vain;
Restless, I'm longing still to meet again.
No Wonder I such mighty Torments prove;
Robb'd of my Happiness, my only Love.   10

Oh! let our fond *Imbrasures* ne'er disjoin;
Rest in my Arms, and lock me fast in thine.
By thee and sacred Love himself, I swear,
My Earthly Paradise, my Heaven is there;
The Souls in other Worlds, and blest above,   15
May learn of thine to *charm*, of mine to *love*.

30. Untitled

Why pants my fondest tender Dove
  With any jealous Fear?
Give up thy Doubts to Me, and Love,
  My Life, my Soul, my Dear.

Think, if from me thy Pain proceeds,   5
  'Tis paid with Interest here;
My Heart within my Bosom bleeds
  For ev'ry falling Tear.

Oh! let me kiss those Eyes of thine,
  Where such sweet Grief appears;   10
Let them pour all their Floods to mine;
  I long to drink their Tears.

Let my fond trembling Arms explain
  My Passion to my Dear,
And, pressing thus, confirm you reign   15
  The only Monarch here.

Thy Form, thy Flame, my lovely Youth,
  Security appears;
Oh! trust my everlasting Truth,
  Nor kill me with thy Tears.   20

31. Untitled

Your kind Example cures me more
Than all your Counsel cou'd before.
I find my Anguish half remov'd,
The Quiet of my Soul improv'd.

No more, my Friend, those Eyes of mine ⎫   5
Now languish for the Sight of thine, ⎬
But with their Native Freedom shine. ⎭
In publick often now I trace
Thy Likeness in some other Face.
Thy chosen Absence I allow,   10
Well reconcil'd to Parting now,
Whose Mention us'd to kill my Heart,
See, gentle Youth, thy wholesome Art.
Love my Companion, and my Friend,
Does on my New-born Case attend.   15
My Eyes, oft fix'd upon the Earth,
He raises up to stranger Mirth.
Strephon has all his Ardour lost,
Oh shall thy Summer meet his Frost!
Some kinder Climate ———chuse,   20
Nor here thy tender Moments lose.
Beat not against this Rock in vain, ⎫
The Marble softens at the Rain, ⎬
Ev'n putrid Marble weeps again. ⎭
But Oh! his Breast is colder far,   25
Than Rocks, or chilly Fountains are;
No more thy Tears, or Numbers flow;
Disdain to shine upon his Snow.

32. Untitled

I chide the Winds, and hate the Air,
That press thy Lips.———I would be there.
Oh hold me fast, let me not part
From those dear Arms———O hear my Heart!
It pleads thy Stay, and in my Breast,
I hear it talk.———O charming Guest!   5
Here pitch thy Tent, nor hence remove,
But feast with me on Deathless Love.

33. *On naming Mrs.* * * * *

O! treat my bleeding Heart with tender Care, ⎫
The Wounds, you lately made, are bleeding there; ⎬
They ake, and fester with inclement Air. ⎭

Not eastern Winds can more destroying prove ⎤
To all the New-born Beauties of the Grove, ⎬ 5
Than that sweet Breath which chills the God of Love. ⎦
Why does it mention that ungrateful Theme;
A Rival's Praise! Do I too tender seem?
And is this, O imprudent Youth! some Art,
To give me back the Freedom of my Heart?   10
———Yes, it will do, and I some Name shall find,
To give an equal Torment to thy Mind:
In Wit, or Fondness, thou art wond'rous poor,
I am too jealous, thou art too secure.

34. Untitled

When Oh! my Stars, when will ye join
My lovely *Strephon*'s Hand to mine.
Oh! when shall I his Bosom claim,   ⎤
Bless'd in his Arms, crown'd with his Name, ⎬
Without an Injury to Fame.   ⎦
Oh! if there cou'd be Fetters found,   5
Stronger than these, I wou'd be bound;
Not that my Heart requires a Chain,
For it can ne'er be free again.
But I, by ev'ry Way, wou'd be
Eternally secur'd to thee.   10
And ev'ry Proof my Love wou'd give,
That thou in Nature canst receive.
Can there a greater Wonder be,   ⎤
Than I, who doat on Liberty,   ⎬
Courting my Stars to give it thee? ⎦   15
Triumph, my Love, on thy own Pow'r,
Fondly increasing ev'ry Hour.
Had Fortune made me ne'er so great,
I wou'd have shar'd thy humbler Fate.
For thee I wou'd have held a Crook,   20
And drank the Murmurs of the Brook.
The gilded Chariot, ne'er so lazy made,
I would resign for thee, and for a Shade;
Dangers and Pains wou'd still appear but light,
To sleep within thy faithful Arms at Night.   25

35. *An Imitation of* SAPHO.
Written by One of her own Sex.

I, alas! have vainly try'd
Fear and Fondness to divide;
Oh! they are too near ally'd.
And I love to that Degree,
They can never part in me: 5
In my very Soul they live,
And a Thousand Torments give.
Oh! Ye sad unsocial Pair,
Who inspire each other's Care;
Have some Pity on a Breast,   10
Yield my Heart a little Rest;
Cruel Tyrant! Will you sway
All the Night, and all the Day?
Must my Dreams have no Release?
Let my Dreams afford me Peace.   15
Let me meet my Dearest then,
At Morning we must part again;
Bus'ness claims my Love too soon;
Sleep within my Arms till Noon.
In my Arms——Oh where dost fly?   20
Let me kiss thy opening Eye;
Rather let my Kisses seal
Their Lids again,——Oh lie thee still,
Till I've prepar'd my tender Heart,
Which does so fondly love,——to part.   25
But oh! I dream, I dream indeed,
Thou art not here,——Oh Heav'n forbid!
Alas! my Soul, where can'st thou be,
Or how imploy'd, if not with me?
What Arms detain thee, Oh that Thought!   30
Has Death, or something like it, brought.
I am alone; perhaps thou art
Now charming of some other Heart.
My little Pillow I have prest,
Inquiring for thy softer Breast;   35
The Wreck of Jealousy I find
Renew its Torments on my Mind:

I rave, I rave, and all I do
Proves that I love, but oh! am jealous too.
Thy Soul and Body both I fear;   40
Thy Soul, thy Heart, thy Mind, thy Ear;
For thee I all Things apprehend,
Thy Enemy, but most——thy Friend.

36. *On* CHRISTMAS *Morning.*
Written by a Young Lady.

Welcome, Morning, to my Sight, ⎤
Thou, To-day, art doubly bright, ⎬
Damon's Eyes assist thy Light. ⎦
Oh! conduct me to his Arms,
Who bestows thee all thy Charms;   5
How would'st Thou or I appear,
Were He not to crown the Year?
On his Bosom I will praise
Thy Beauties, in diviner Lays;
I will too thy Sweetness sing,   10
Mortals shall believe thee Spring;
And the Birds in Concert join,
As on their lov'd *Valentine.*
Here alas! I do thee Wrong:
Fond Impatience spoils my Song: 15
He will give redoubled Fire,
To my Soul, and to my Lyre:
From thy Sun how could'st thou shine,
Or I sing, now wanting mine?

37. Untitled

My longing Bosom wish'd to throw
It self into your Arms below,
Forgetful cruel Death wou'd meet
My bleeding Heart, ere it cou'd kiss your Feet;
Or that thy generous Breast wou'd dare,   5
To take my Fate, and perish there.
That killing Thought alone restrains
My eager Arms, and makes me drag my Chains.

Better, far better, it will be,
To suffer all Things than to murder thee.　　10
In Death we shou'd our Tenderness betray
My gushing Blood to thine wou'd force its Way;
And in the thoughtless Agonies of Death,
My Lips wou'd draw in thy departing Breath;
My shatter'd Arms wou'd their Imbracements hold,　　15
Ev'n after Life, when the poor Clay was cold.

38. *To Mr.--------on his having resolved to write no more.*

By CLIO.

In vain I for a Reinforcement stay'd,
　　The Muses all are thine, *Apollo* too;
Once the bright God pursu'd a flying Maid,
　　But I, alas! a flying God pursue.

In vain I turn my Darling *Shakespear* o'er,　　5
　　Thence to extract the Sweetness I admire;
But he converses with my Soul no more,
　　Silenc'd, like me, by thy superior Lyre.

To thee the Muses all their Bounty gave,
　　They're sweet, they're flowing, and they're
　　　　nobly Strong;　　10
Musick's thy Friend, and Fancy is thy Slave,
　　Giving immortal Beauties to thy Song.

Whom shall I court? Oh! what shall *Clio* do,
　　To tune her artless Numbers for thy Ears?
Clio, tho' bolden'd by such Praise from you,　　15
　　Is lost, and trembles with Confusion here.

My Thoughts thy higher Genius does controul,
　　And all within my Bosom now lie bound;
They us'd to pour too fast upon my Soul,
　　And, till this Moment, ne'er forgot to sound.　　20

Oh! had I equal Forces, and cou'd break,
   Revoke it strait, thy most ungentle Vow.
Oh! write again; if only for her Sake,
   Whom thou hast fetter'd up to Silence now.

What mighty Wonders thy sweet Muse performs!   25
   What all the Language of my Tongue confines;
My Words are Prisoners to the matchless Charms,
   And feels the Pow'r of thy victorious Lines.

Stay yet, our Frozen Climate to improve,
   Awake our Spirit with thy charming Lyre,   30
Inform us how to sing, and how to love;
   Nor let the Soul of Harmony retire.

To other Worlds, great Star, arise,
   When this thy noble Business is compleat;
Shine on my Numbers from thy Native Skies,   35
   And warm my Soul from thence with thy own Heat.

39. Untitled

To *Aberglasney*, lovely Place!
Let the Muses bend their Race;
Where their gentle Favourite lies;
See, with what enamour'd Eyes,
They survey his Face and Mein,   5
And the Soul that shines within.
Some the deathless Wreath prepare; ⎤
Some adorn his flowing Hair;   ⎬
All are pleas'd and busy there. ⎦
Here he charms the list'ning Woods;   10
Here he tunes the murmuring Floods,
Who, alas! in vain essay
To imitate his softer Lay.
Flying Birds suspend their Wings,
While the lovely Poet sings;   15
Happy Herdlings, whom his Lyre
Do with Tenderness inspire:
Happy Grottos, where his Mark

Shines upon the yielding Bark.
They grow amorous, while they bear 20
Damon's tender Numbers there.
Happy Maid, whoe'er thou art,
Who can touch so sweet a Heart!
Time can do thy Charms no Wrong,
Shining still in *Damon*'s Song. 25
Here the Ecchoes sing his Name,
And the Birds repeat his Flame.
He informs the Flocks to bleat,
Who lie list'ning at his Feet,
And forbear to play, or eat. 30
See his gentle Dog is pleas'd,
Rage and Hunger are appeas'd;
And he lies with starting Ears,
While the charming Strains he hears.
Charming Numbers! I cou'd praise 35
Everlastingly his Lays.
See the God of Numbers shines,
In his Form, and in his Lines;
Pen and Pencil, he attends,
Every deathless Stroke befriends. 40
Happy *Gronger!* favour'd Brow,
Thou art grown *Parnassus* now.
Cooper's *Hill*, divinely sung,
Will eternally be young.
Gronger Groves as firm shall stand, 45
Planted by thy Infant Hand.
I shou'd too immortal be,
If I once were sung by thee.
But believe me, tuneful Swain,
I retire with racking Pain. 50
Trust me, I wou'd rather be
Still a Poetess and free,
Ranging the Wilds of Verse with thee.
Let thy Verse adorn my Name,
Gentle Shepherd, give me Fame; 55
For I now the Bay resign,
And no longer hope to shine;
Youth and Love, and every Muse is thine.

Houshold Cares, stupid Friends,
The *Hymenial* God attends: 60
I must leave thee; but I will
Oft in Soul attend thee still.
When, the Candles burning blue, ⎤
Aerial Forms appear to View,   ⎬
I will pay my Visit too.   ⎦   65
For our fetter'd Clay is said,
By the Witty, to be dead.
When lov'd Liberty is lost,
What's the Body but a Ghost?
Empty Shades of what we wear,   70
If we've witty been, or fair.
From this Letter, some dull *Prude*
Too severely will conclude;
But I trust it to your Eyes,
Where no mean Conclusion lies.   75

40. *To* -----------.

From Love and Anger for a while set free,
Careless I lie, like one becalm'd at Sea;
The Tempests, which had made my Thoughts run o'er,
Are hush'd within my Soul, and rage no more.
Love swell'd th' unruly Tide, alas! too high,   5
And now my Thoughts, like ruin'd Shipwrecks, lie;
My Hopes and Fears, and the dear Cause I see
With Unconcern, and owe the Change to thee:
Hereafter I shall dully gentle prove,
Like thee, an arrant Slumberer in Love.   10

41. A PASTORAL SONG.

Ye Trees, you gentle Canopy,
That shaded once my Love and me;
Now bending, hear my Sorrows plain,
Nor lift your Branches up again.
                                          Derry, &c.

Once, as your Leaves, my Heart was free,   5
Or, as your Winds, at Liberty;

'Till Love, that sweet Destroyer, came,
To blight my Hours.————He was to blame.

Derry, &c.

Upon this very Bank we lay,
This Bank be ever green and gay;   10
This Bank be dress'd in blooming *May*,
Tho' I dissolve in Tears away.

Derry, &c.

Ye tender Osiers, as ye bend
And trembling thus my Grief attend;
As you to one another twine,   15
Say, thus the Lovers Arms did join.

Derry, &c.

Oh! Did you mark his gentle Care,
When he beheld my Bosom bare?
What a respective Kindness shown,
And how he warm'd it with his own?   20

Derry, &c.

His Lips my Hand all trembling press'd,
While speaking Tears his Flame confess'd;
For Talking was too mean a Way,
Tears only can such Souls convey.

Derry, &c.

And Oh, ye little heedless Flock,   25
That griefless feed on yonder Rock!
With Pity your sad Mistress view,
Who, happy, us'd to pity you.

Derry, &c.

How oft my Shepherd, for my Sake,
Was wont your tender Lambs to take,   30
And fold them to his lovely Breast,
Where I had only Right to rest?

Derry, &c.

My Love was good to every Thing,
To all the Plants that, careless, spring;
His Hand the nipping Frosts remov'd,   35
And with its Warmth the Flow'rs improv'd.

Derry, &c.

How oft he did from Winter's Rage
Protect the Linnets in the Cage!

Himself the happy Prisoners feed,
And charm them with his tuneful Reed!   40
Derry, &c.

Ye Trees and Plants and budding Flowers,
Witnesses of our softer Hours,
Go back again, refuse to bring
Your Sweetness to the coming Spring.

Derry, &c.

But if you will, in Spite of me,   45
Wear Nature's gaudy Livery;
Yet grant this Favour from your Bloom,
When I am dead, to deck my Tomb.

Derry, &c.

And you, dear Earth, his Print retain;
Defend it from the beating Rain;   50
And oh sweet Tree! this Boon I claim,
To bear my Lover's sacred Name.

Derry, &c.

Afterword

In the preface i suggest that the poems by the anonymous lady constitute the most vital and interesting sequence of love poems in English between Shakespeare's sonnets and Hardy's *Poems of 1912–13*. The aims of this Afterword are to justify such a claim through detailed discussion of specific poems and of the sequence as a whole, and, by means of stylistic comparison, to assess further the case for Martha Fowke's authorship.

In vain I to the Dead return

In the opening lyric of the series, "On Reading Dr. Donne's Poems," the poet finds not only Donne wanting, but also Cowley, Waller, Lansdowne, Congreve, Addison, and Prior. It is mischievous of her opening line to imply that all these writers were dead, since Lansdowne and Congreve, perhaps also Prior, were still living at the time it was written;[1] but, as a literary judgment, not without point. What these poets lack, she declares in the adroitly varied refrain which ends each of her stanzas, is "Tenderness." In presenting this confident appraisal she shows knowledge and insight as well as audacity. According to A. J. Smith, "by the early eighteenth century Donne was a dead issue, a historical specimen only."[2] The anonymous lady's poem is an exception that proves the rule. Not only does she take Donne seriously—and as a love poet rather than as a satirist—but she displays both a keen critical sense of his amatory verse and a subtle ability to refine his versification. The poem highlights several key qualities of her writing: it is spirited, independent, and witty.

For this poet, what is wrong with the love poems by the famous writers—all male—whom she has cited is an excess of "Wit and Art" (10). She points the criticism directly in the succinct line, "All Conceits my Flame would wrong" (21). This is to charge her

86

forerunners—by implication especially Donne, probably also Cowley—with an over-ingenuity that betrays the feeling it is supposed to express. The charge is sharpened by the finesse with which she shifts the meaning of the word "art" from its sense in lines 7 and 10, where it signifies poetic skill, via line 25, where it means "contrivance," to denote cunning or artfulness in the final stanza (49). Despite this criticism, she shows she has read Donne attentively by employing a nine-line stanza, used by him in ten of his love poems but uncommon in the eighteenth century except in Spenserian imitations.³ In keeping, nevertheless, with her protest about excessive art, she does not intersperse different rhymes and line lengths as he does. Instead, her smoother versification allows a nicer irregularity. In two of the poem's six stanzas she alters the position of the triplet in her rhyme scheme: moving it from its regular place, in lines 5–7, so that it ends the second stanza and begins the fourth. These metrical grace notes finely intimate not only her skill but her individuality.

Such a blend of self-assurance and accomplishment is a hallmark of the anonymous lady's writings, and it is nowhere better illustrated than in poem 19, "On Being Charged with Writing Incorrectly." Eighteenth-century women writers often complained, with good reason, that they were denied educational opportunities open to men, and that, with special injustice, they were then criticized for ignorance or artistic ineptitude.⁴ "On Being Charged with Writing Incorrectly" is a spirited retort to the latter accusation; at the same time, it wittily undermines male assumptions of superiority based on learning. Not only does the writer display verve and skill in language and metrics alike, but she roundly condemns the education to which men of her own rank were subjected.

That education was often brutal. Richard Busby, glanced at in lines 15–16, was a former headmaster of Westminster School who was famed not so much for teaching as for flagellating his pupils. The poet charges that such treatment did them as little good intellectually as physically, for the result is that they have been schooled into methods which for her are tedious and deadening. While other contemporary women often objected, rightly, that they were enslaved by law and custom, she slyly transfers the notion to men whom she calls "Slaves of *Busby's* nod" (15). She presses the point home by painting a ludicrous picture of the god

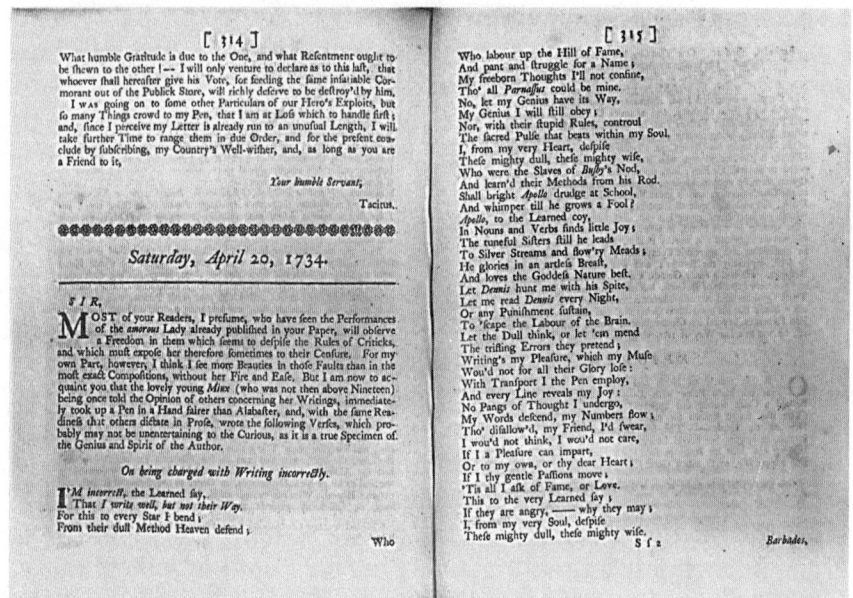

Pages 314–15 of volume 1 of *Caribbeana*. Reproduced by permission of the Syndics of Cambridge University Library.

Apollo, patron of poetry and music, undergoing an education which would have rendered even him stupid. It is not grammar which is important to poetry, she argues, but "the Goddess Nature" (24). She therefore restores Apollo to his proper place as leader of the Muses—the "tuneful Sisters" of line 21—among the "Silver Streams and flow'ry Meads" (22) of their traditional home on Mount Helicon. In a way that is characteristic both of the poem and of others in the sequence, these graceful classical allusions show at the same time that she herself is very far from uneducated. As the next line indicates, she has read the most famous critic of her time, John Dennis. Indeed, she amusingly claims that she would rather read Dennis, notorious for bile and aridity, than learn grammar by rote.

But the poem's main thrust is to celebrate her independence as a writer. Though she is nothing if not confident—"all *Parnassus* could be mine" (8)—she is not prepared to trade her freedom for the kind of fame which in her time, she suggests, can only be gained by following fixed rules and methods. She demonstrates her individuality through the mocking phrase in which she refers to Parnassus, sacred to Apollo and the Muses, as "the Hill of Fame" (5); and she goes on to disparage authorities on writing and criticism. This airy, even cocky, dismissal of experts and specialists dominates the first two thirds of the poem. What is more startling, however, is that she follows it by appealing to the motive of sheer enjoyment:

> Writing's my Pleasure, which my Muse
> Wou'd not for all their Glory lose:
> With Transport I the Pen employ,
> And every Line reveals my Joy.

(31–34)

She writes, she says, because she likes it; and this valuing of poetry for the delight it gives is perhaps her most subversive point. At a time when women were taught chastity and submission, she claims her own will and desire as proper motives for poetry. If this carries a hint of erotic pleasure—"Transport" means rapture or ecstasy—it is wholly in keeping with her address to the "Friend" whose enjoyment she cherishes as much as her own. Not only does she wish to move her friend's "gentle Passions," but, discreetly, she names "Love" as her object, along with this "Fame," limited to two people, for which she is prepared to settle (41–42).

Here as elsewhere, the anonymous lady presses her case as much through the expressive resources of her verse as through her witty, often paradoxical, arguments. She exploits her chosen form, iambic tetrameter couplets, with fluency and dash, often deliberately—even ostentatiously—repeating the kinds of "incorrectness" which would have brought her criticism. She begins, therefore, as she means to go on, by highlighting her insouciance about rules: the poem's first word ("I'm") is a jaunty elision, and the opening line is unconventionally run on. This is to suit verse to sense with a vengeance, a ploy she repeats to even more arresting effect a dozen lines later. Here her refusal of constraint is dramatized, again, by enjambment, and then by a ten-syllable line to end the couplet, as if her "Genius" overflows the metrical scheme: "Nor, with their stupid Rules, controul / The sacred Pulse that beats within my Soul." This kind of skill, and wit, belies the word "artless" which she uses later (23): it is the kind of art that conceals itself. The handling of the verse is not only artful, but directly pertinent; and this suggests that she is not so much breaking the conventions as teasingly stretching them, and displaying her own powers in the process. She works mainly in concise syntactic units of one or two couplets, only twice extending to three; she reverses the opening foot of occasional lines for expressive variation; she uses enjambment between couplets only lightly; and her rhymes are consistently firm and decisive. This is not the verse of an incorrect writer, but of one who both knows the rules and how to bend them aptly.

The poem's energy stems from its buoyant, often almost colloquial, diction as well as from its lively verse. Most of its words are plain and monosyllabic, and it does not disdain elision, as in the opening word already mentioned, and, later and just as surprisingly, in the contraction "Writing's" (31). Indeed, part of the poem's attraction is its air of spontaneous, excited speech. "No, let my Genius have its Way" (9), says the poet, as if talking directly to critic or (as it later turns out) sympathizer; and she attacks her rivals and opponents with pungent informality: "I, from my very Heart, despise / These mighty dull, these mighty wise" (13–14). Here the word "mighty" nicely hovers between orthodox and slang usage: the wise are powerful but dull, indeed very powerful and very dull. The same is true of the word "stupid" with which she has just qualified the rules she despises. According to the *OED*, the first recorded use with the sense "tiresome" dates from 1778, so the primary meaning is probably "Belonging to or characterized by stupor or insensibility." Nevertheless, it would be unwise to rule out an earlier instance of the more popular sense, not least because this fits so well the tone of exasperated mockery. It is in part through her use of expressions normally deemed low in polite verse of the period that the poet taunts her critics. She ends as informally as she has begun, with a colloquial employment of the verb "may" that omits the expected infinitive, and by repeating her most scornful gibe as if by way of a refrain. At the same time, her shift from "Heart" (13) to "Soul" (45) when she repeats the couplet underlines how passionately she feels her defiance.

Part of the poem's freedom probably derives from its private, even intimate, mode of address. The "Friend" to whom the poet appeals in line 37 was probably the man with whom she was in love;[5] but the poem does not necessarily suggest that he was the only reader she envisaged. Indeed, the frame of reference cannot merely be private, for the writer also enters deftly into contemporary public debates about nature and artifice in poetry. The key text for those debates, which she must have known well, was Pope's *Essay on Criticism* (1711). However, while Pope argued that "Those RULES of old *discover'd*, not *devis'd*, / Are *Nature* still, but *Nature Methodiz'd*,"[6] this poet shifts the emphasis away from "Method" (4) and towards "Nature" (24) unqualified. Elsewhere in his *Essay*, Pope remarks that "Great Wits" may "*snatch a Grace* beyond the Reach of Art" (152, 155), but here the poet appeals to inspiration ("The sacred Pulse" of line 12), and a "Genius" (9–10) which is her own and which she is determined to follow. Again, while Pope would later boast, in *An Epistle to Dr. Arbuthnot*, of his precocity in versification: "I lisp'd in Numbers, for the Numbers came" (128),[7] she anticipates him with a claim which, the fluency of her verse suggests, is no exaggeration: "No Pangs of Thought I undergo, / My Words descend, my Numbers flow" (35–36).

The anonymous lady claims the right to exercise her genius in a tour de force of sparkling writing which demonstrates a bold command of her chosen verse form and a keenly personal view of the expressive and critical issues at stake. Along with other poems by women of the period, including Mary Chudleigh, Lady Mary Wortley Montagu, Sarah Egerton, and Mehetabel Wright, "On Being Charged with Writing Incorrectly" destroys the myth that eighteenth-century verse is characteristically formal and lacking in passion. Yet the poem could hardly have displayed such freedom and informality had it been written for publication. The pity is that, for a young woman of standing, much more decorous verse was necessary if she was to establish herself as a writer. Ironically, what enabled the freedom and informality of this poem was its necessarily limited, though intimate, audience.

The pity is all the greater because the anonymous lady also shows, elsewhere in the sequence, that she was both informed about and capable of taking part in public dialogue concerning other social and literary questions. One example is her interest in pastoral, the convention that both provides the setting for many of her poems and is clearly related to her advocacy of a "natural" kind of writing. Pastoral had a special appeal to female

writers of the period, probably because it offered an accepted
form not only for amatory verse, but for poems which could ex-
plore broader questions of love and courtship and imagine an al-
ternative social order.

To write pastoral at this time was to enter the controversy be-
tween what J. E. Congleton has called the "neoclassic" and "ra-
tionalist" traditions. These had been represented by the
pastorals of Pope and Ambrose Philips respectively, first pub-
lished in the same volume in 1709; the "rationalist" theory was
set out at length by Thomas Tickell in five celebrated papers of
1713 in *The Guardian*, and mocked by Pope in a *Guardian* sev-
eral issues later.[8] Among the poems assigned to the anonymous
lady, only one, "To the Same. A Pastoral" (poem 4), locates itself
centrally in the convention. Yet the poem avoids both the "neo-
classic" and the "rationalist" path. Unlike most pastorals, it has
the woman woo the man. Indeed, inclining neither to Pope's kind
of pastoral nor Philips's, it exploits the form as a means to ex-
press female affection and desire, and to imagine a world free
from masculine "Business" (8, 10). This is a version of pastoral
distinctive enough to have contributed to the form's develop-
ment. But, because it is an intimate love poem by a woman, it
had to remain private, and therefore, like so much other verse by
women of the period, outside the literary margins.

"On a Fan Presented" (poem 8) illustrates further the special
kind of spin which the anonymous lady was capable of giving to a
currently popular topic. Fans, which were often richly decorated,
were fashionable both in themselves and as objects of comment,
as the many references in *The Spectator* indicate. It was in *The
Spectator*, in 1711, that Addison published his entertaining essay
on "the training up of young Women in the *Exercise of the Fan*,"
and Pope, in the following year, his poem about a fan-painting of
the story of Procris and Cephalus.[9] Pope later published his
poem as an imitation of Waller, and it probably looks back to an
epigram on a fan by Francis Atterbury which was thought to
have perfectly matched Waller's style.[10] Whether or not this is so,
Pope's poem seems to have stimulated Gay to write an entire
mock-epic on the subject, *The Fan* (1713), which in turn influ-
enced *The Rape of the Lock*.[11] The anonymous lady treats the
theme quite differently.

She opens the poem with a flourish echoing Gay's mock-heroics: "Not the *Trojan* triumph'd more, / When the Golden Fleece he bore."[12] Yet the next couplet immediately shifts the register to intimate polite talk: "My Hand, with equal Pleasure, takes / The Gift thy tender Friendship makes." While Gay's poem, like *The Rape of the Lock*, sets out to satirize what it defines as female vanity and pride, the anonymous lady's goes on to characterize the various uses of the fan, as if in neat metrical emulation of a *Spectator* paper. The fan can not only "raise" but "prolong Discourse"; after an outburst of affected rage it "drowns the Jarring of the Tongue"; and, able to show "Tenderness" as well as "Scorn," it can both "give Denial to the Fool," and "curb the Bold, inspire the Cool" (12–18). Yet the poet ends by modulating to another note again. She turns from this brief, playful catalogue to an expression of devotion to her lover which, without quite dropping the humorous tone, is plainly in earnest. In the poem's twenty-six short lines she has redefined a topic used by men of the time for compliment or satire as a vehicle for witty imagination and affection.

In other poems, too, the anonymous lady fulfills her promise in her poem on reading Donne by demonstrating not only wit but "Tenderness." Poem 6, "His Picture," and poem 10, "The Appeal," evoke the lyrics of Waller and his imitators through their accomplished versification, their ability to sustain an extended metaphor, and their glowing tributes to the beloved. Where they differ is that, as in all of her work, the artistry has the effect not of calling attention to itself but of heightening the expression of passionate feeling. Part of the explanation for this difference is that, unlike amatory verse by men, written for the admiration of other men as well as—though not necessarily—for their addressees, her poems focus more directly on the lover and on her relationship with him. The effect is to reclaim what had become a male tradition and turn it to other purposes.

In "His Picture" the poet asks Cupid to use his dart as a paintbrush to portray her lover. This conceit allows her to single out various features of her lover's face for description and admiration; yet she ends by accusing herself of lacking art to do justice to his actual appearance: "*Damon*'s Picture is more charming, / It has painted in my Heart" (27–28). "The Appeal," a poem of reproach, follows a parallel strategy in that it emphasizes not so much her lover's lack of constancy as what she calls, in a telling pun, her "heavy Truth" (19). The metaphor on which this poem is built is that of the law court—especially appropriate if her lover, like many clever and ambitious young men of the period, was studying law. She maintains the image with a chain of apt but unobtrusive legal expressions, and brings it to a climax in the final stanza:

> Hold up thy Hand, oh! much-lov'd Swain,
>   While the poor Plainant pleads;
> And know, while I thy Heart arraign,
>   My own with Sorrow bleeds.
>
> (25–29)

This represents a quite different approach from that of the many love poems by men which stress their own suffering in an attempt to gain sexual favor.

"His Picture" and "The Appeal" also show how well the poet handles different types of quatrain, a form often practiced by male writers of amatory verse, particularly because it lends itself well to musical settings. The stanza just quoted, which is in the form often known as the short quatrain, is adroit in its choice of rhyme words, its matching of syntax to structure, and its occasional metrical variation, as in the uneven movement of the first line and the reversed first foot of the second. "His Picture" is more unusual in that the meter is trochaic rather than iambic, and all the even-numbered lines are catalectic. The effect of this deft technical device is to keep arresting the lyrical falling movement of the longer lines and so bring the reader up short. This not only adds structural compactness, but sets expressive statement before harmony. Poem 13, "Song," in the same stanza form, illustrates the same principle and in doing so partly belies its title. Though the poet shows great skill by rhyming all the even-numbered lines on the same vowel, the effect is not simply one of euphony but of contrast with the challenges and declarations on which she has the poem turn, as at the end of the third stanza: "Grow a more obsequious Lover, / Or no longer think of me" (11–12).

I BURN MY PEN, I BITE MY NAILS

Many of the anonymous lady's poems show the "Tenderness" which, in her poem on reading Donne, she argues is necessary in amatory verse. An equally striking contribution to the canon of English love poetry is, however, a quite different kind of feeling and expression. In two poems from late in the sequence, "A Letter to My Love. —— All Alone, Past 12, in the Dumps," and "To My Love" (poems 21 and 25), she conveys a sense of dramatic response and engagement for which few earlier love poems in English outside Shakespeare's Sonnets offer any precedent.

This sense stems from the vivid informality of her language, the ease and panache of her versification, and, above all, from her ability to build into the structure of the poems the twists and turns of passionate thought and feeling. "A Letter to My Love" flaunts its scorn for decorum with the "low" word "Dumps" in its title, and with two colloquial elisions at its turning point: "And, now I think on't," "to ha' staid" (26, 28). Until line 33, when the poet is expressing not so much her grief at being parted from her lover as her anger and frustration, the style is sharp and racy: "I write and blot, and write and burn" (16), "I burn my Pen, I bite my Nails" (22). The urgent tetrameter couplets also help convey a strong sense of spontaneity through their use of the line unit, as in the two examples just quoted, and through occasional telling breaches of the line and couplet boundaries:

> Wine in this sullen Moment fails;
> I burn my Pen, I bite my Nails,
> Rail at my Stars, nay, I accuse
> Even my Lover, and my Muse.
>
> (21–24)

This vivid impression of a mind swerving through a chaotic set of feelings and responses culminates in two reversals. So unexpected is the first of these that it seems to arrive in the very act of writing. Having tried, without success, reading, versifying and drinking in an attempt to calm herself, she has reached an impasse that provokes her to blame not only her fate and her muse but her lover. She asks a question that is initially no more than an expression of her anguish—"Why did he let me go, I cry"— and then realizes that it is not necessarily rhetorical: "—And, now I think on't, tell me why?" (25–26). This astonishing volte face brings her to recognize that she could have stayed the night with him. But, instead of heightening her resentment, it produces

an equally striking change of direction, this time emphasized by
the poem's only formal variation, a triplet:

> The Night was rainy, and the Wind
> To all thy softest Wishes kind.
> For thee and Love methought it blew,
> As if my parting Pains it knew,
> As if it was a Lover too.
>
> (29–33)

Again the emotional logic is wholly convincing, for the thought of
the wind leads her to fear that, while she is "safely shaded" from
its power (34), it may be threatening him.

The last third of the poem, beginning at line 40, displays an-
other of the qualities that make the anonymous lady's work so
distinctive. Poem after poem of the sequence refers to her own
body and her lover's; indeed, few other love poems in English
show so intense a physical imagination. Here, her concern for
her lover's safety leads her to express all the more sharply how
much she is missing his bodily presence: "thy Bosom" (46), "thy
Voice" (48, 49), "thy dear lov'd Hand" (50), "thy Eyes" (52). The
poem ends in a stunning climax which rises out of this tangible
sense of absence, as she imagines him visiting her in spirit and
herself meeting him in kind:

> This Hour, when pallid Ghosts appear,
> Oh! cou'd it bring thy Shadow here;
> I every Substance wou'd resign,
> To clasp thy Aerial Breast to mine;
> Or if, my Love, that could not be,
> I would turn Air to mix with thee.
>
> (54–59)

As Jerome McGann has put it, "the desire for actual physical
contact is so imperative—the need for the 'substance' of her
lover—that she physicalizes her own dissolution in order to
imagine an erotic encounter."[13] The final image of physical/spiri-
tual conjunction packs an erotic charge that is all the more com-
pelling for its subtlety.

Poem 25 presents the impact of parting rather than absence,
but demonstrates an equal ability to dramatize passionate emo-

tions and responses. The emotions are powerfully mixed, for the poet's love and longing struggle with her anger and resentment at her lover's coolness. Again the command of verse form and expressive language is crucial to the poem's effect. The form is a six-line stanza of iambic pentameters, rhyming ABABCC. Four of the five stanzas consist of a single, forcefully managed, compound sentence; all five end with a couplet that sums it up or gives a further twist to the argument; and each couplet also exploits a tellingly varied refrain. The diction and syntax do not employ colloquialism, as in "A Letter to My Love," but they are often packed with implication. Adjectives and nouns are combined to forge a keen paradoxical edge in "sad Society" (3), "kind Excess" (19), and, most of all, *"artful Tenderness"* (21); a simile that compares the poet's words to traitors forsaking her carries an accusing hint for her lover (9); and the only fully-developed metaphor is held back for maximum effect to the start of the final stanza ("Bid the rude North be gentle to the Spring").

The poem's most arresting achievement is to convey with unsparing directness the bitter and painful feelings brought about by a crisis in the relationship. This is epitomized by the fourth stanza, which is its turning point:

> While I was griev'd to such a kind Excess;
>   Oh! how untimely must thy Prudence be,
> To bid me *meet, with artful Tenderness,*
>   *The Arms that were no Friends to Love or thee.*
> Beware how you instruct me in that Part,
> Lest I give him the true, and thee the faithless Heart.
>
> (19–24)

The lover's advice, here thrown back at him by the poet, implies that she was either already married or required to show favor to an unwelcome suitor. Elsewhere in her poems she uses the word "Tenderness" and its cognates to define what it is to love. By coupling it with the epithet "artful," she brings out how cruelly she feels betrayed by his apparent complacency. She clinches the stanza with an apt and striking application both of closing couplet and refrain, exploiting the one to counter tartly that she might take him at his word, the other to provide a new and hostile qualifier for the word "Heart." The final line gains added keenness from its extra foot and from its pointedly antithetical construction.

My Lyre, which once my Freedom sung

For all the fire of its response, this poem, like others which challenge her lover, ends by devoting herself to him. Although one of the anonymous lady's themes is freedom, and although she consistently displays her individuality, the poems also show her sacrificing freedom, self, and even poetry to love. Indeed, she expresses confidence in her future as a poet only to shrug off such ambitions. In poem 16, "To the Same," she declares: "The God of Verse himself appears, / And promises my Name / Shall brightly shine in future Years," only to continue: "But what is Life, or Fame?" (21–24). This sad bravado gives way to regret elsewhere, as in poem 12, "The Absent," when she complains: "My Lyre, which once my Freedom sung, / Now groans beneath my Chain" (11–12); and, with rueful irony, imagines people asking what has become of her: "Is this the Muse the Men admire, / And whilom call'd a *Wit*? / Has the *South-Sea* undone her Lyre?" (21–23). Even these qualms have disappeared by the end of the untitled poem 20, in which she expresses total devotion to her lover:

> My Heart, for Numbers never staying,
>   Flies almost in Prose to thee;
> And the God of Love, obeying,
>   Thinks not of my Fame, nor me.
>
> (39–42)

At this period writing could, just, offer a woman a chance not merely to express and define herself but to live more fully, for example by taking on the social identity of a recognized poet which, in all the lines quoted above, she sees slipping away. A crucial question raised by the poems is therefore how she could have brought herself to sacrifice so much.

It is not simply that a woman who published love poems compromised her reputation—unless, like Martha Fowke in *The Epistles of Clio and Strephon*, she insulated them with artifice.

For this woman, the problem went deeper. For example, when she declares in poem 3, "To the Same," "while I write, *I live*," she does not mean writing as an act of self-assertion, but, quite specifically, the power which writing about her lover gives her (7–8). This places in a different light her insistence on setting her subject above her art. When she asks, in poem 15, "To Damon," "But why do I his fragrant Bosom Wrong, / With Similes that only grace my Song?" (21–22), there is no sign that she is protesting too much in an attempt to call attention to her poetic finesse. On the contrary, when she introduces a variation into the same poem's rhyme scheme a few lines later—a quatrain among its couplets—the point is to foreground his "peculiar Art," and what amounts to her total subjection:

> Oh! who can say which Sense he pleases most?
> He has peculiar Art to touch them all:
> Not Virtue's self its Icy Pow'r can boast;
> The Soul and Body hastens to his Call.
>
> (27–30)

The poem breathtakingly ends with her drawing on the myth of Pygmalion to imagine not her own creative power but her lover's:

> I tremble, lest the Paper, I've convey'd,
> Itself be warm'd into some happy Maid;
> Cou'd the cold Statue kindle into Fire?
> What wilt thou do, who burns with my Desire!
>
> (37–40)

In the explosive last line she addresses the poem she is sending him, fearing not that her writing, but that the desire he excites, may transform it into a rival. So bold an expression of the force of sexual desire is extraordinary in the verse of a woman writer at this period. Indeed, one of the distinctions of the sequence as a collection of love poems—a distinction it shares with Shakespeare's Sonnets—is a repeated stress on the power of desire to crush and overwhelm the self completely.

Despite the anonymous lady's subjection to her lover, her verse does not endorse the normative assumption of the time that, as a woman, she is necessarily entitled to less power and liberty than a man. In poem 18, "To the Same," she seems to cast herself in a conventional role of female passivity, assigning all initiative to the male. She asks, for example: "How does the languid *Cynthia* look, / Till *Phoebus* makes her fine?" (7–8). The sun and moon were, of course, stock symbols for male dominion and female passivity. But the object of this question, which the poem repeats in several different forms, is to emphasize a dependence on her part to her lover which she not only finds galling but exploits as an argument to require more of him. When she declares: "Think not my Passion long can live, / Without the Warmth of thine" (3–4), she not only accuses him of failing her but threatens him with the loss of her love; and the poem ends with her imagining a "Haven" in another man's heart. At the core of the poem is anger and frustration at a loss of control which she cannot help and which she would do almost anything to redeem: "By Heaven's! I long for Liberty, / And only for an Hour" (23–24). She laments the loss of her freedom both because she values it highly and because she cannot help sacrificing it.

Nevertheless, for all her resistance to the constraints of law and custom, the anonymous lady could not overcome the social and ideological forces which disadvantaged her as a woman and empowered her lover as a man. One reason why she was able to escape the limitations of amatory verse by her male contemporaries is that she was taking genuine risks in contesting those forces; and what her poems achieve at their most intense is to highlight contradictions between poetry, freedom, and love which could not exist for well-born men.

Poem 14, "The Protestation," defines a conflict between love, poetry and different rules of conduct for the two sexes. It begins by showing that she cannot even be sure her poems will reach her lover, because "cruel Prudence" (5) may require their destruction, presumably for fear of discovery from parental or marital vigilance. A male poet, entitled by his gender to greater personal liberty, would not have suffered such a restriction; indeed, tradition would have licensed him to write poems not only of love but seduction. Not surprisingly, she finds the constraint inhibiting, despite her gifts as a poet and her unconventionality—as shown by her startling use of the word "brilliant" as a verb in her first line. But the difficulty is more complicated still, as she realizes through comparing herself with her most famous predecessor. Sappho, sanctified as a woman writer of love poems, was able to celebrate her lover in her verse, and to win glory by doing so. But the anonymous lady, so passionately in love that she can only write love poems, finds that a taboo on writing to or of her lover all but prohibits her from writing at all: "But from the only Object I'm confin'd, / That can give Love or Glory to my Mind" (13–14). The result is conflict between her "Genius" for poetry and her "Hopes" for love (16). And the only consolation she can envisage is at best a sad swap: on the one hand love, and the devotion of her lover; on the other, her chance to win fame as a poet, her peace of mind, the limited freedom she possesses, and indeed all her potential as a human being. The poem is both a demonstration of her powers as a love poet, and a discovery that, because she is already having to surrender them, only the same kind of ardor from her lover will compensate: "Oh! give me Love for all that I have lost" (16).

An even more striking dramatization of the conflict between love and poetry is poem 22, "Occasioned By Some Lines of His." Here the poet again suggests that her hopes for fame and recognition are fading, but this time the implications are even worse, because she has found that her lover writes poetry too. The opening stanza reproaches him for having hidden his light under a bushel, while regretting the decline of her own fame as his aspirations grow. In the following stanzas, however, she seems to reassert herself, not only through her graceful and witty verse, but through an argument which aligns his kind of poetry with hers. The reason his verse is so good, she says, is that it is, like hers, inspired by love and therefore natural and "artless" (41). Echoing "On Being Charged with Writing Incorrectly," she rejects the rules and methods which at this period were supposed to govern the writing of poetry, and also the classical education through which they were taught. Love is a better mentor, she claims, than Busby (23–24). This seems a good way of re-establishing her own position as a poet, since she has not only inspired her lover but set him an example. She brilliantly caps the point at the end of the sixth stanza: "They for thy Master will enquire, / Say, *'Twas a Mistress tun'd thy Lyre*" (35–36), playing on the sense of the word "Mistress" both as female lover and as instructress. As Isobel Grundy observes, this is "to assert the superiority of the kind of naturalness that was so often identified with (and condescended to) in female poets." But again, as Grundy also recognizes, there

is a heavy price to be paid.[14] Although the poet can enjoy herself
in ridiculing the "odious Rules" (37) of conventional writing and
the "heavy Luggage" (39) in which they are packed, the effect of
her lover's verse, even though inspired by her, is only to enslave
her more fully. The last two lines, and the sentence which fol-
lows, effect a Faustian bargain in which she gives up all to a lover
who now seems to her all-powerful:

> With this the Victory is whole,
> And I deliver up my Soul.

Sign'd and Seal'd in the Presence of the God of Love *and the* Muses.

The poems about parting which end the sequence suggest that
this was no exaggeration. Although, as I have shown, poem 25 is
also combative and accusing, all express utter dedication to her
lover.

FAME THEY SOUGHT, BUT LOVE I SEEK

Whatever her own fate, the anonymous lady in a real sense
sacrificed her poems. Their content made it impossible for her
to publish, perhaps even retain, them; and in sending them she
surrendered to her lover the power to do with them as he saw fit.
As a result, there is no way of knowing whether the twenty-six
poems in *Caribbeana* represent all the verse she wrote to him.
In particular, none of the poems seems to represent the love af-
fair at its beginning or in its early stages; and for this reason any
narrative they yield must be incomplete. There is, however, evi-
dence that some of the poems are arranged to provide thematic
and narrative continuity. Part of this evidence is the publishing
of groups of up to six poems at a time in single issues of the *Ga-
zette*, and part the way in which the series begins and ends.

"On Reading Dr. Donne's Poems" is an apt choice to open the
sequence because it is, in effect, a manifesto for a new kind of
love poetry to challenge the prevailing masculine tradition. The
two pairs of poems which close the series owe their position not
only to thematic logic such as this but to narrative order: all ei-
ther foreshadow or respond to the lover's departure and the in-
creasing threat that the affair is ending. The last poem of all

strikes an especially convincing and poignant note with its terminal image of the lover forgetting the poet by falling in with the boisterous merriment of his comrades: "——— Thy Friends will of thy Tenderness complain, / And Wine and Wit will raise a Laugh again" (22–23). The mockery of "Tenderness" is bitterly ironic, in light of the key role played by the word in the opening poem and in several others.

Of the remaining poems, which make up the main body of the series, seventeen were placed in groups of between three to six per issue, and four appeared one at a time. Though thematic or narrative continuity is possible among the four poems published in single issues, it is not to be expected, because they were separated by intervals of between four and six weeks. Indeed, the three poems placed on their own late in the sequence clearly do not follow narrative order. Poem 22, "Occasioned By Some Lines of His," in which the poet responds with surprise to her lover writing in verse, cannot have been written after the untitled poem 20, in which she reassures herself with a poem he has written for her; and, similarly, poem 21, "A Letter to My Love," would fit better a few steps later in the sequence, because it anticipates the themes of parting and separation in the two pairs of poems that conclude it. Nevertheless, two of the later poems in the series do appear to be placed in chronological order, though not consecutively. Poem 19, "On Being Charged with Writing Incorrectly," seems to reflect a settled period in the relationship; and, as I have suggested above, it is echoed by poem 22, "Occasioned By Some Lines of His," which culminates in the poet giving herself up to her lover completely.

The poems grouped in single issues show the most coherence and continuity. The first group, poems 2–4, aptly follows the opening poem of the sequence because in different ways each of these also addresses the theme of writing. But there is little evidence in any of the first four poems about when in the affair they were written, or in what order, except that poem 3, "To the Same," indicates that it has already lasted a year (20). There seems little in common between the next group printed together, poems 5–8, except that all are in some way occasional: the first responds to the lover's illness, the fourth to his gift of a fan; while the second imagines his picture, and the third is written on one of his letters. The group which follows, however, the largest of all with its six poems, shows both narrative and thematic coherence, at least in the first five. Poem 9, "To Mr. * * * * * *," an anguished reproof at the lover's inattention, is followed by "The Appeal," in which the poet pleads that she observes the laws of love better than he does; poem 11, "The Complaint," which expresses her misery when apart from her lover, both represents a thematic development of the first two and introduces its successor, "The Absent"; and poem 13, "Song," provides an appropriate conclusion for all five by restating her despair in his absence, regretting her lost liberty and reaffirming her own fidelity. Only "The Protestation" (poem 14) seems out of place, since its main theme links it to other poems, including those in the first group, about writing. Finally, the remaining group, poems 15–18, also shows some narrative and thematic coherence. The opening poem introduces the theme of love in excess; poem 16 elaborates on this, and, in conjunction with the following poem, expresses absolute commitment to her lover and indifference to other men who court her; while the fourth in the group, poem 18, brings it to a dramatic close when, though "blind with Love" (1), the poet recognizes that her lover is losing interest, regrets her lost freedom, and imagines finding a better "Haven" for her "Ship-wreck'd Fondness" (26–28).

While the twenty-six poems do not show a consistent narrative line, they possess strong thematic integrity, and they contain several patterns of change and development that give them coherence as a series. It is these qualities, especially the first, which require them to be valued not only as independent poems but as a sequence. The defining issue of that sequence is what it meant for a woman of the period, known for her poetry, to write poems of love.

And the God of Love, obeying, Thinks not of my Fame, nor me

The fact that the poems in *Caribbeana* constitute a sequence is relevant to Phyllis Guskin's claim that they were written by Martha Fowke. As I have mentioned in the introduction, Fowke contributed to one sequence of love poems, *The Epistles of Clio and Strephon*, and wrote at least one other, the poems in *Clio* addressed to Aaron Hill. Although it is not always easy to keep stylistic and other evidence separate, this closing section considers the case on stylistic grounds for Fowke's authorship.

Guskin establishes two points in favor of the identification by observing that "tender" is not only a favorite word of Fowke's, but that it and its cognates occur frequently in the poems of the anonymous lady; and by citing several examples in Fowke's verse and that of the anonymous lady of the rhyme "impart"/ "heart." She also remarks parallel images in each body of work— the poet's faithful dog, the poet with her eyes cast down in melancholy; similar themes, especially that of lost liberty; and a shared taste for expressions which present the act of writing in physical and sensual language.[15] To this evidence may be added the use of the word "herdlings" discussed above, and also that of the relatively uncommon term "atom," which occurs in the work of both writers.[16]

Although these stylistic and thematic clues are quite telling, not all evidence of this kind supports the identification. For example, one striking feature of the anonymous lady's verse is its formal versatility and dexterity. Of the twenty-six poems assigned to her in *Caribbeana*, nine are in tetrameter couplets, six in pentameter couplets, six in quatrains, four in six-line stanzas, and one in an unusual stanza form of nine lines. The poems also show considerable invention and variation in handling these forms. Six of the nine in tetrameter couplets are in iambic meter, and three in trochaic; three of the nine include triplets; and two include pentameter lines at important points for extra effect, in one case as the final line of a triplet. Triplets also occur in four of the six poems in pentameter couplets; while the four poems in six-line stanzas, two of which rhyme all their lines alternately, and two of which close four alternately-rhymed lines with a couplet, all use different combinations of meter and line length.

More detailed textual analysis, beyond the scope of this edition, would bring out the full metrical verve of these poems. The verse known to be by Martha Fowke does not, however, show quite the same level of formal excellence. First, there is less variety in her choice of metrical forms. Of the seventy-three poems and fragments which may be firmly assigned to her,[17] no fewer than fifty are in pentameter couplets, the staple form of the period for serious verse; fourteen are in tetrameter couplets; three are in quatrains; and the remainder are in stanzas of different lengths—four of six lines and one each of five and eight lines.[18] It is possible to argue that one reason why Fowke's verse shows less metrical variety is that some of it was written for publication at a time when formal regularity was in favor.[19] Thus all the verse letters in *The Epistles of Clio and Strephon* are in pentameter couplets, as are four of her five poems in Hammond's *Miscellany*, and six of her nine in Savage's. Conversely, there is more formal variation in the poems addressed by Fowke to Hill, which, like the poems of the anonymous lady, are very unlikely to have been written with publication in mind. Even here, however, a fairly high proportion of the verse is in pentameter couplets. Twenty-five out of a total of forty poems or fragments are written in this form, while nine are in tetrameter couplets, four are in six-line stanzas, one is in eight-line stanzas and one is in quatrains. Both in her tetrameter and pentameter couplets, Fowke regularly exploits the variations of triplets and occasional longer lines—especially in *The Epistles of Clio and Strephon*, in which she uses both more than her co-writer William Bond. But, although the verse acknowledged as hers is never less than accomplished, it does not display quite the same energy and invention as the verse assigned to the anonymous lady.

A further line of enquiry concerns the other female-authored poems published in *Caribbeana*. The group of five printed in a single issue, poems 30 to 34, are of special interest because they are ascribed to a young lady who, Keimer's correspondent claims, was later praised for her verse, and because, albeit in miniature, they constitute a sequence—like the poems not only of the anonymous lady, but those by Fowke in *The Epistles of Clio and Strephon* and in *Clio*. The five show stylistic and thematic affinities both with the poems attributed to the anonymous lady and with verse known to have been written by Fowke. The theme of the poet's lost liberty, and of longing for her lover's embrace, occur three times in the five poems (though not in the same three); and the word "tender" appears in another three (in poem 33, twice). Other evidence, however, links the poems more specifically with the anonymous lady's, as distinct from those published as Fowke's. The phrase "my lovely Youth" occurs both in poem 23 and in poem 30; and further parallels are the threat to reputation (poem 34) and the need for emotional security (poems 30 and 34). Though not quite expert in their versification, the five poems also show a metrical invention which resembles that of the anonymous lady. Of the four in couplets, two include triplets, one even beginning with a consecutive pair; a third, written mostly in tetrameter, shifts to four pentameter lines at the end; and poem 30, the only one in quatrains, parallels poem 13 by using the same sound for the "B" rhymes throughout.

The remaining nine unassigned love poems also show stylistic and thematic affinities either with verse known to be by Fowke, or with the poems by the anonymous lady, or with both. Six use the word "tender" or its cognates; four express longing for the lover's arms; and two display unusual freedom in their versification—poem 37, which is untitled, moving from tetrameters into pentameters, and poem 35, "An Imitation of Sapho," not only shifting from trochaic to iambic tetrameters but opening with a triplet, breaking several lines with emphatic pauses, and climaxing in a pentameter: "Proves that I love, but oh! am jealous too" (39). But the most striking evidence is an idea which appears in two of the poems by the anonymous lady and in one of the poems which are unassigned. In poem 5, "Occasioned By His Illness," the anonymous lady exclaims: "Our Lips in the last Gasp shall join, / I'll catch thy Soul and give thee mine" (30–31); and in poem 26 she asks her lover to do the same for her: "Oh! bring thy Bosom to support my Head, / And catch my Soul e're it too far is fled" (8–9). Poem 37 employs an identical image when the writer imagines herself dying with her lover: "And in the thoughtless Agonies of Death, / My Lips wou'd draw in thy departing Breath" (13–14). In *Hydriotaphia: Urne-Buriall* (1658), Sir Thomas Browne summarized the belief these poems invoke when he remarked of "the ancient Gentiles": "That they suck'd in the last breath of their expiring friends, was surely a practice of no medicall institution, but a loose opinion that the soul passed out that way, and a fondnesse of affection from some *Pythagoricall* foundation, that the spirit of one body passed into another; which they wished might be their own."[20] But the immediate source was probably either Dryden's translation of a passage in Virgil's *Aeneid*, Book 4, where Dido's sister speaks as Dido lies dying on her funeral pyre, or Pope's "Eloisa to Abelard." Dryden's lines are: "Bring Water, bathe the Wound; while I in death / Lay close my Lips to hers; and catch the flying Breath" (982–83); Pope's,

"See my lips tremble, and my eye-balls roll, / Suck my last breath, and catch my flying soul!" (323–24).[21] The fact that these poems use the same idea may suggest that they are by the same author.

There are, then, significant thematic and stylistic parallels between the poems by the anonymous lady and those which are unassigned. Several solutions to the question of attribution are therefore possible: the anonymous lady may have written some, even most, of the other poems as well as those credited to her; or, as Phyllis Guskin has argued, Martha Fowke may have written all forty as well as the one ascribed to Clio; or, again, it is conceivable that some of the poems are by Fowke and others by one or more unidentified authors. Anyone who has worked on women writers even of the recent past knows how difficult they can be to track down; and it is especially difficult to distinguish work by different authors who belonged to the same coterie. A case in point is the identity of the female contributors to Savage's miscellany and their addressees. The three contributors— among them Fowke—write in a similar style. One of them has yet to be identified, along with two of the addressees, who were implicitly also writers.[22]

An alternative approach to the question of attribution is to look for difference rather than similarity. This can be particularly useful when studying a group of texts dealing with the same themes in which some are of known authorship and some not. The final part of this afterword therefore juxtaposes three pairs of poems: two about parting, two written late at night, and two about the lover as a writer. In each case, one of the poems comes from the group assigned to the anonymous lady, and has already been discussed in detail; the others are, respectively, a poem by Fowke from *Clio*;[23] the unassigned poem 28 from *Caribbeana*, "Written at Midnight"; and the single poem in *Caribbeana* attributed via her pen-name to Fowke.

The poem from *Clio*, reproduced in Appendix B, is entitled "On the Sad Thought of Parting." It closely parallels "To My Love," poem 25 by the anonymous lady. First, the two poems outline situations which are painful for other reasons beside separation. When Fowke exclaims: "Insensible this bosom might have laid, / Dully contented in cold lawful Arms" (27–28), she almost certainly refers to her marriage to Arnold Sansom which had taken place a year or two before the poem was written.[24] The other poet evokes a similar predicament when she reproves her lover for asking her to *"meet, with artful Tenderness, / The Arms that were no Friends to Love or thee"* (21–22). Whether the arms in question belonged to a husband, or, as Keimer hastened to reassure his readers, to an unwelcome suitor, the scenarios of the two poems are very alike. The crucial difference is that the poem by the anonymous lady challenges her lover in a way that the poem in *Clio* does not.

A second way in which the two poems correspond is that they employ the same verse form—a six-line stanza of iambic pentameters, rhyming ABABCC—and in much the same manner. Neither has any stanza run into the next, and the only obvious difference in the versification, except that they do not use the same number of stanzas, is that, while the first tends to exploit the final couplet as a syntactically and semantically distinct statement, the second makes it a refrain. In other ways, however, the two poems differ markedly. First, as I have shown above, the poem assigned to the anonymous lady is strikingly direct and dramatic. Fowke's, on the other hand, is more profuse, even literary. Not only does it contain many adjectives, some supporting personifications characteristic of eighteenth-century verse (such as "smiling Hope" and "soft Relief" in line 5), but it employs an extended simile (the "lost lavish Heir" of stanza 2 who becomes a "Bankrupt" in stanza 3); and, in the final stanza, an extended metaphor (the "happy Villager," content because he has never known "the fine Desires of Life"). The simile of the bankrupt heir, and some of its phrasing, recalls some of the sonnets of Fowke's favorite writer, Shakespeare;[25] so too does the pun, untypical of eighteenth-century writing, in the phrase "my Soul's sole Estate" (line 16). If these two poems are by the same writer, they speak with quite different voices.

The second pair of examples is poem 28, "Written at Midnight," and poem 21, "A Letter to My Love." Both, again, are written out of very similar situations: each expresses a sense of desperate, sleepless misery. The main differences are stylistic. Essentially, the unassigned poem is more prolix and conventionally literary. Its use of adjectives often lacks precision, and is also at times over-insistent, as in the phrases "long wintry Night" (1) and "melancholy hopeless Love" (41). This, and the large number of exclamations, gives the poem a histrionic tone akin to that of some of the other unassigned poems, especially the untitled poem 37. Similarly, the two mythological allusions misfire—the first, "The happy Sun in *Thetis'* Bosom lies" (37), because it is bathetic, and the second, to Prometheus (50–51), because it is hyperbolic. The control of syntax, and its coordination with the verse line, is also slack. Twice the poet resorts to awkward inversions, in lines 32 and 39; and once to one of the expletives which Pope deplored in his *Essay on Criticism* ("Does" in line 8).[26] The end-stopped pentameter couplets contrast especially sharply with the pungent tetrameter couplets of "A Letter to My Love"; and the diction of the two poems differs equally—the one predictable, the other raw and racy. Although "Written at Midnight" manages a sudden change of direction in line 17, this is less arresting than the dramatic twists and turns of the other poem; indeed its whole structure is much less dynamic.

Nevertheless, there are two clear links between "Written at Midnight" and other female-authored love poems in *Caribbeana* and elsewhere. First, the reference to "Bays" in line 18 suggests that the writer already had a reputation as a poet, and parallels similar remarks not only in several poems by the anonymous lady but in some of Fowke's poems in *Clio*, as well as in the untitled poem 39 beginning "To *Aberglasney*," which is probably by Fowke.[27] Second, the idea of suicide again connects the poem to the untitled poem 37; and the poet's highly unorthodox desire to try her fate in another world also associates it with poem 36, "On Christmas Morning." This set of connections suggests that the poem may be by the same writer as some at least of the other unassigned poems; and it leaves open the possibility that, whether or not she also wrote the poems assigned to the anonymous lady, she could have been Martha Fowke. The difference between the two poems is not only one of voice, as in the first pair of poems compared, but also of quality. If the same poet wrote both, the difference is a reminder that not even good poets always write well.

The third pair of examples consists of poem 22, "Occasioned By Some Lines of His," and poem 38, "To Mr. -------- on His Having Resolved to Write No More." Here the basic factors in common are that each was written by a woman who had already won a reputation as a poet, that each demonstrates the skill and sophistication of her verse, and that each addresses a man whose

own verse is the poem's main subject. In the first poem, respond-
ing to the discovery that her lover is also a poet, the anonymous
lady not only declares that she loves him all the more, but surren-
ders herself to him entirely. In the second, attempting to dis-
suade her addressee from giving up writing, Fowke praises him
lavishly. Although these scenarios are not quite the same, the dif-
ferences are largely over-ridden by a similarity in each poet's re-
lation to her subject. While the anonymous lady ends her poem
by devoting herself wholly to her lover, Fowke portrays herself as
chained, bound, imprisoned, conquered—above all, silenced—by
her friend's poetry, and implicitly also his other attractions.

The main differences between the two poems are in style and
tone. "Occasioned By Some Lines of His" is deeply personal and
intimate, expressing an alarming sense of the writer's vulnera-
bility to her lover. The diction of Fowke's poem is more conven-
tional, more public; and this helps place it within the convention
of complimentary verse that characterizes much of Savage's
1726 miscellany, to which she, Hill, and Dyer all contributed. The
convention allows tributes of absurd extravagance, as in the
stanza which elevates the addressee above Shakespeare; and
phrases such as "immortal Beauties" (12), "Soul of Harmony"
(32), and, perhaps most of all, "great Star" (33), which rise into
the rhetorical stratosphere. At the same time, Fowke also seems
to protest too much what she claims is her own inferiority. No
one reading this poem, or indeed other verse by her, could apply,
as she does, the epithet "artless" to her versification (14); and
the poem itself bears witness that she is anything but silenced
(20, 24) by the other's lyre, however "superior" (8) she declares it.

Although the two poems are very different, it is still by no
means inconceivable that both were written by Fowke. Indeed,
the mischievous wit and eroticism of the stanza which opens the
poem by Clio offers a link with several of the poems assigned to
the anonymous lady. Fowke's transposition of Daphne's role with
Apollo's both suggests that her pursuit of the addressee is not
just literary but amorous, and, at the same time, parodies the
traditional reading of Daphne as a symbol of chastity. This re-
calls the arch, teasing tone in some of the poems by the anony-
mous lady, and also her deft use of mythological allusions, like
the one to Pygmalion in poem 15, or to Apollo and Daphne them-
selves in poem 20. Despite these similarities, however, the poem

ascribed to Clio must at the very least have been written out of a different position, or a different kind of relationship, from the anonymous lady's.

The purpose of comparing these three pairs of poems has been to demonstrate some of the stylistic questions at issue in the attribution of verse by one or more anonymous women in *Caribbeana*. Other pairings would, of course, produce different results; in particular, I have underrepresented the verse in *Clio* which strikes the same notes of devotion and abjection to the lover as some of the poems assigned to the anonymous lady. However, while I hope others will pursue comparisons between alternative combinations of poems, it is impossible to have full confidence in attribution on stylistic grounds—or even in documentary sources such as *Caribbeana*, when research has not yet succeeded in verifying their evidence independently. The problem, and also the challenge, is how to interpret such evidence as there is, both literary and historical. Some of the findings set out in this edition support Phyllis Guskin's contention that the anonymous lady was Martha Fowke. But they do not all point one way; and it is possible that further research will lead to a different ascription, even to the discovery of a previously unknown writer.

If Fowke did write these extraordinary poems, she was an even better poet than is apparent from the work for which she is so far known. The poems that she is known to have written do not speak in the same voice as most of the poems assigned to the anonymous lady. But poets do not always adopt the same patterns of expression, and the stylistic range of her accredited verse is already quite wide. The crucial fact is the existence of the poems. Whether or not they claim a place among the works of Martha Fowke, they certainly deserve one in the canon of English poetry.

Appendix A: Introductory matter from *Caribbeana*

THIS APPENDIX IS ARRANGED IN THE FOLLOWING ORDER: (1) EXTRACTS from the Preface to Volume 1 of *Caribbeana*; (2) introductions to the poems of the anonymous lady; (3) introductions, where they exist, to the other female-authored anonymous love poems.

1. FROM THE PREFACE *[normalized from italics to roman]*

What we now offer the Publick is of the Growth and Produce of one of our Sugar Colonies, in *America*, and being the first of the Kind imported from that remote Corner of the Globe, at least so well preserved, it will be no Wonder if the Curious of all Ranks and Degrees should be enquiring after, and desirous to make some Trial of so rare a Commodity. But to be more explicit. The following Miscellany is carefully selected out of a Paper which was carried on by Subscription, several Years in the Island of *Barbados*, being published once at first, and afterwards twice a Week, for the Amusement of its Inhabitants; and where we may perceive the Liberty of the Press has been claimed and generally allowed, in the same just and legal Latitude we hope it will ever continue to be in their Mother-Country. (1:iii)

The judicious Reader will observe, amongst the Productions of these last, several that are of a lighter Sort, and less Importance than others; and which consequently he will ascribe to different Pens. Of this Kind, for the most Part, may be reckon'd (beside some in Prose) the Essays in Verse that are interspersed throughout. These may be ranged under two Heads; such as are on common and indifferent Subjects, and those that bear an Allusion to particular Incidents arising on the Place at the respective Seasons in which they were composed. As to the former, 'tis presumed, they are equal, if not superior to most that have been published in other Miscellanies, and well received. [. . .] They give Variety to the whole, and may besides be a principal Entertainment to the Young of either Sex, and such as are

113

of a gay and airy Turn, who do not care to be confined to serious and intense Studies, and who yet ought not to be entirely neglected in an Undertaking designed, in some Degree, to please all. Nor will it be amiss to hint here that such of the Poetical Performances as are not introduced by Letter, or otherwise, are yet all along printed without any Mark of Separation betwixt them and what goes before, although they are quite distinct and independent; the Reason of which was that the respective Papers might be only distinguished as when they first came out in *Gazettes*. But perhaps it may be needless to take Notice that a few of such as had no Relation to Dates are removed from the Places they originally held, for the Sake of lengthening some Papers which might otherwise look too short; a Method we were led to by the Poverty of some of the *Barbados* Prints (not at all to be wondered at) from whence we could pick but very little fit for our Purpose, and we did not care to lose what was.

But we cannot drop the *Poetry* of this Collection without distinguishing a considerable Number which were wrote to a Gentleman of *Barbados*, by a Lady then living here (since deceased) and whom to name, would be an additional Credit to the Work. Such of her Productions as have already appeared in any other Shape, have been much called for, and greatly admired by the best Judges. These which were in no other Hands till they first came abroad in the *West-Indies*, are certainly not inferior to any of them; and if we may take her own Opinion for it, which we have seen in a Letter to a Friend of her's, they are some of the best she ever wrote. But as they would probably have soon been utterly lost, were it not for this our Care, so it may perhaps be a Pleasure to her Acquaintance (which was very extensive) to trace her Pen where they could little expect to find it; and which, 'tis apprehended, several will be able to do. However, she is not the only Author of the fair Sex, to be found in this Miscellany, which is all we think convenient to say, at present, on that Head. Several other Copies of Verses there are, of a different Sort, which though composed here, were also first made publick from the Original Manuscripts by the only *Press* that ever was known in any of the *Caribbee Islands*; and which we shall now leave to speak for themselves. (1:viii–ix)

To conclude. This Collection might, we are sensible, have appeared to more Advantage, if a *certain Gentleman*, now in these Parts (and whose Pen at first visibly contributed towards it) had been pleased to lend us his Assistance; but as he had, no doubt, his own Reasons for declining thereof, yet without opposing however, or discouraging the Undertaking; so if we are not much deceived, the Generality of our Readers will notwithstanding find here, upon the whole, what will give them both Profit and Pleasure equal to their most sanguine Expectations. (1:x)

2. Introductions to the Poems by the Anonymous Lady

Wednesday, July 18, 1733.
SIR, · *July* 16, 1733.
Love is undeniably the most powerful of all our Passions. It carries every Thing before it, and makes all other Considerations give Way and submit to its Dictates. It takes Possession of the wisest as well as the weakest Minds, and often occasions the like* Effects in both. It renders the Coward brave; the Miser, generous; the Meek, angry; the grave, gay; the dull, witty; the rude, polite; and turns the Man of Business at once into a Man of Pleasure. In a Word, tho' we cannot easily describe this Passion, it appears to be the same in all Ages, at all Times, and in all Climates. That the other Sex are equally susceptible of it with our own, is certain; and that they are generally more constant may, I believe, be fairly admitted, notwithstanding they are so often rally'd by the Men for their suppos'd Fickleness. But be that as it will, my Design at present is only to introduce the following little *Piece*, compos'd by a young Lady, after she had been occasionally dipping into Dr. *Donne*'s Poems, which seems to have put her on imitating that Author's Manner and Measures, without carrying her from her own Favourite Subject, whereon she must be allow'd, I presume, to write pretty feelingly. The Lines, being never yet in Print, may not, perhaps, be unacceptable to your Readers of Taste, tho' it is not expected they should give equal Pleasure to others, as to the Gentleman to whom they were several Years ago address'd, and who, being now on the Spot, could, if he pleas'd, I know, embellish your Paper with many other Productions of the same Kind. (1:182–183, introducing poem 1, "On Reading Dr. Donne's Poems")

*The D. of *Rochefoucauld* says, in his *Moral Reflections*, that a Man of Sense may love like a Madman, but never like a Fool.

Wednesday, November 28, 1733.
From my CHAPEL.
Having lately obliged the Learned, I now hope to please the lovely Part of my Readers, by inserting the following *Pieces*, which were wrote above Twelve Years ago, by one of their own Sex, who made a considerable Figure in the *Beau Monde* at Home. The *Poems*, which

have never been in Print before, were addressed, on different Occasions, to the Object of the Author's tenderest Affections, who, 'tis said, is, and has been some Time, in this Island; and, if I guess right at the Gentleman, the Lady is no more to be wondered at for her Passion than she can be discommended for her Taste. But this, it seems, must be a Secret, which, if discovered, would at once deprive me of the Expectations I have of being often favoured with some of the politest Compositions that can possibly adorn my Paper. (1:247, introducing poems 2–4, "To * * * * * * * * *," "To the Same," and "To the Same. A Pastoral")

Wednesday, February 7, 1734.
As several of my future Papers will probably be filled with Matters of a more serious and publick Nature, I intend to dedicate this to the Service of the Ladies, by presenting them with some other Pieces of the amorous Fair one mentioned formerly, who has long since distinguished herself amongst the finest Writers in Poetry. They are all addressed to the same Gentleman, and there is no Reason therefore to question but her Passion was as steady as it appears to be ardent. How well she has painted it, they are the best Judges who have ever been in the like Circumstances; but I must declare I think there is a peculiar Softness in the Verse, and a Tenderness in the Sentiments, which are hardly to be met with in any of the best Performances of those of our own Sex, on the same Subject. These Manuscripts were, I understand, put into the Hands of a Friend of mine, to dispose of, as he should think proper, with these Restrictions only from the Owner (who is now, it seems, a Man of Business) that *Names* be concealed, and that he did not by publishing them at any Time postpone what might be of more immediate Service to the Island. For my Part, I have Reason to rejoice that having often been obliged to my Fellow-Labourers in *Europe*, by borrowing from their Weekly Papers, I am like to be able to return the Favour; since they will, no doubt, readily enough transcribe from me what cannot but be acceptable to the politest Readers of the Age. (1:264, introducing poems 5–8, "Occasion'd by his Illness," "His Picture," "Written on one of his Letters," and "On a Fan Presented")

Saturday, March 2, 1734.
It is a particular Satisfaction to me, that, thro' the generous Assistance of Friends, I am able to relieve the Fair Part of my Readers, from shocking and melancholy Subjects, by presenting them with ingenious Performances on a Topick which cannot but be agreeable to them, and I hope, at the same Time, not unacceptable to those of my

own Sex: *Love* is, no doubt, a noble and useful, as well as a delightful Passion, and ought therefore, on no Account, to be discouraged, provided it be placed on proper Objects; such I mean as will admit of the Gratification of it, without displeasing our Maker, or injuring any of our Fellow-Creatures. The following Poetical Pieces are Originals from the same soft Hand with those formerly inserted in this Paper, and are also addressed to, or occasioned by the same happy Gentleman, whose Name, as I have hinted before, must, with her's, be religiously concealed. They are wrote at different Times; and, tho' the Spirit of them seems to be pretty equal, yet, 'tis plain, the Poetess was not always in the like Humour, but discovers thereby that she felt the Anxieties and Uneasinesses that are said to attend even the most successful Amours.———I flatter myself, that if this Paper be sent out early enough to wait on the Ladies with their Chocolate (as I intend) it will be no disagreeable Entertainment, after the very elegant one they will have met with, over Night, at *Pilgrim*; where the excellent Letters on *Justice* have, I understand, procured the *Barbados Gazette* the Honour of being constantly taken in. (1:276, introducing poems 9–14, "To Mr. * * * * * *," "The Appeal," "The Complaint," "The Absent," "Song," and "The Protestation")

Wednesday, 20 March, 1734.

> *Pity, Truth, Justice, Openness of Heart,*
> *Courage, Politeness, Eloquence, and Art,*
> *The gen'rous Fire with which Ambition flames,*
> *And all th' unsleeping Soul's divinest Aims,*
> *Touch'd by the Warmth of Love, burn up more bright,*
> *Proud of the Godlike Power to give Delight.*

Hill.

Tho' I am now in the Decline of Life, and my Constitution is pretty much worn with the Cares and Troubles of it, I will not be ashamed to acknowledge that I still retain the utmost Veneration for the Ladies; free, however, from an unchaste Thought, or a loose Desire. Their Persons and Characters are always sacred with me, and nothing therefore shall come out of my Mouth, or drop from my Pen, but in their Favour. The Truth is, I apply to the whole Sex, what Mr. *Pope* says of *Belinda*, in his *Rape of the Lock*;

> *If to her Share some Female Errors fall,*
> *Look on her Face, and you'll forget them all.*

'Tis for this Reason that I have determined whatever may hitherto have escaped me, thro' the Artifice of any Correspondent of more Wit than good Nature (and who might possibly have a secret Meaning, which I was not aware of) nothing shall be inserted in the *Barbados Gazette*, with Regard to that delightful Part of the Creation, which will admit of the Possibility of a Construction to their Disadvantage.

Having made this Apology (which, perhaps, may be thought unnecessary) I shall proceed to give further Evidence of my Inclinations to oblige them. *Monsieur de Voltaire*, in one of his Letters concerning the *English* Nation, lately published, tells us, 'That the Ladies who adorn the Theatrical Circle at *Paris*, as well as those at *London*, will suffer *Love* only to be the Theme of every Conversation.' If this be justly said of the two politest Cities in the World, it is not improbable that our own little Spot may bear some Proportion in the same Account; and, if what is contained in the Motto of my Paper be true, it is no Reflection at all to suppose it. Nor can I by any Means think what the Author I have already nam'd relates, in the same Book, of the renowned Sir *Isaac Newton*, *That he never had any Commerce with Woman*, any Addition to his Character.———But, be those Things as they will, I'm perswaded the following Pieces taken from the Stock of Manuscripts, out of which I have already more than once fill'd a *Gazette*, will not be an unacceptable Entertainment for this Day, since the amiable Poet continues to sing in Notes as soft as the Passion she describes, and with a Constancy which seems perfectly agreeable to the Divine Institution. (1:290–91, introducing poems 15–18, "To Damon," "To the Same," "To the Same," and "To the Same")

Saturday, April 20, 1734.
SIR,
Most of your Readers, I presume, who have seen the Performances of the *amorous* Lady already published in your Paper, will observe a Freedom in them which seems to despise the Rules of Criticks, and which must expose her therefore sometimes to their Censure. For my own Part, however, I think I see more Beauties in those Faults than in the most exact Compositions, without her Fire and Ease. But I am now to acquaint you that the lovely young *Minx* (who was not then above Nineteen) being once told the Opinion of others concerning her Writings, immediately took up a Pen in a Hand fairer than Alabaster, and, with the same Readiness that others dictate in Prose, wrote the following Verses, which probably may not be unentertaining to the Curious, as it is a true Specimen of the Genius and Spirit of the Author. (1:314, introducing poem 19, "On being charged with Writing incorrectly")

Saturday, June 1, 1734.

From my CHAPEL.

Lest the above should be thought to smell too much of the Counting-House by some of our Readers, we have subjoin'd another Piece from the *Fair-Fountain* which has so often entertain'd them. There have been great Inquiries concerning the *happy Man*, on whom so much Female Incense is bestow'd, but to no Purpose. However, as this Performance will help us to one Circumstance, *viz.* his being himself no Stranger to the Muses, so I am now able to add another, which is, that he has been in the Island at least seven Years. (1:335, introducing poem 20, untitled but beginning "To my Breast thy Verse applying")

Saturday, June 29, 1734.

The following Poetical Epistle, from the ingenious Lady so often mentioned in this Paper, I have before me, in her own Hand-Writing. It is directed exactly as I have printed it; which my curious Readers, I presume, will not be displeas'd to see. (1:360, introducing poem 21, "A Letter to my Love.———All alone, past 12, in the Dumps"; original italics converted to roman)

Wednesday, July 24, 1734.

SIR,

It has been observ'd that there is hardly a young Lover, of any Spirit or Genius at all, how much soever he may have been a Stranger to the Muses before, but will attempt *the Poet* in Praise of his Mistress, and in Order to set forth and describe the Sincerity of his own Passion. Whether this proceeds from the Analogy there is betwixt Personal Beauty, and the Harmony of Numbers, or, that the Passion raises the Man, and lifts him, as it were, above himself, or that he thinks plain Prose too mean and unworthy of such elevated Subjects, or rather, that he is in Hopes of making Merit, and proposes, thereby, the more easily to gain the Fair; or from all these together, or what other Considerations, I shall not pretend to determine. I must, however, take Notice, that a fine Copy of Verses, a tender Song or Madrigal, has often produc'd Wonders that Way, especially with Ladies of Taste, and been no less effectual even, than a lac'd Coat and Hat, a fine Horse and Furniture, getting drunk, breaking Windows, firing Pistols, or the like pretty Recommendations, and prevailing Acts of Gallantry. You have already been given to understand, that the Favourite and humble Servant of the amorous Heroine, with whose Performances you have occasionally embellished your Paper, was not barely a cold Prose-Writer, and I now send you a Piece she wrote on her having first discover'd it; which may serve as a Proof of what I just now advanc'd, and also be no ill Entertainment, perhaps, to the better Part of your Readers, who will, I hope, be so good as to excuse, for the present, my with-holding the other. (1:366, introducing poem 22, "Occasion'd by some Lines of his")

Saturday, November 9, 1734.
SIR,
I don't know how it comes to pass, but it is observable that our Island has afforded fewer Instances of Heroick Love than may be met with amongst the same Number of People in other Parts of the World. The Male Part of the Inhabitants of this little Spot seem to be entirely bent on Interest with Regard to Matrimony, while yet in other Respects they are, perhaps, as negligent of it as those in *Europe*. We no sooner hear of a rich Widow than we are told of half a Dozen young Gentlemen that have already made, or intend to offer their Addresses to her, leaving, at the same Time, many a lovely young Nymph to pine away the best of her Days without an Opportunity of answering *the Question*. Some, indeed, have endeavour'd to account for what I speak of, and to impute it, to the easy and frequent Opportunities our Youth here have of quenching a vicious Flame with those of a different Complexion, and I wish there was not too much Ground for the Suggestion, altho' it would be still a greater Reflection to suppose them not to possess Souls capable of so noble a Passion as that I am adverting to. There is something, methinks, in Love, when fix'd on proper Objects, and prosecuted with Innocence, which does Honour to our very Beings, as it certainly produces the most beneficial Effects to Society by refining our Manners, and disposing us to every Thing that is human; and tho', like all other Sublunary Enjoyments, there is a Mixture of the Sour with the Sweet, and the Parties, at times, feel great Uneasiness, as well as the utmost Delight, on Account of the Anxieties they are subject to, and the Disappointments they meet a Thousand Ways, yet all these never fail to be thought over-ballanc'd by the mutual Endearments that pass betwixt the Parties, and the Joy and Gladness of Heart resulting from thence. You have often taken Notice of a Lady on the other Side the Tropick, who was far gone in this Passion, and inserted several of her Performances which sufficiently prove it, some whereof intimate that a Gentleman (now amongst us) who was happy in her Affections had also celebrated his own Passion and the Charms of his Mistress in some excellent Pieces of Poetry. This, I am sensible, has rais'd the Curiosity of your politest Readers, who expect to see them, and to have the Pleasure of comparing one with the other; in which Particular 'tis not

improbable they may hereafter be gratify'd, when the Reasons also may be given for concealing them so long. At present, however, I will send you two more Scrips of Paper in the Hand-Writing of the *Fair*, which you must allow me to set a Value upon, and which I desire you therefore to deal as gently by, as if she herself were present; and that you'll return them without the least Spot, or Mark of your *black Apartment*. (2:5–6, introducing poems 23–24, "To Damon" and "To my Love. Wrote in Tears")

Saturday, March 1, 1735.

From my Chapel.

My Friend whom I formerly mentioned to have had several Manuscripts delivered him by a Gentleman of his Acquaintance, assures me that the two following Pieces were wrote by the same *Female Wit* to whose Pen the Publick has been already obliged for divers other Performances of the like Kind, and which were not originally intended for the Press. I am very apt, 'tis true, to be prejudiced in Favour of every Production of the Fair, and always incline to give their Works the Preference, when left to my own Liberty. But as the *Barbados Gazette* has the Honour to kiss the Hands of the nicest and most accomplished of either Sex in this Part of the World (some whereof I may presume to assert are scarce to be matched elsewhere) I would be extremely careful not to offend even the most rigorously virtuous, and therefore must acknowledge a Scruple that at first stuck with me in relation to one of the Poems I now venture to send abroad, which was the true Reason of my not doing it sooner. I was indeed apprehensive that the *Fourth Stanza* might be construed so as to infer a *Criminal* Amour betwixt the Parties, which ought by no means to be countenanced, or encouraged, tho' 'tis certain such Things will now and then happen while Men and Women continue to be what they were some thousand Years ago. However, on further Consideration, the Hint which occasioned my Suspicion, appears to be no more than a Caution the Lover had suggested to his Mistress, on Account of his not being so acceptable to her Relations as another Gentleman who made his Addresses to her at the same time; and I do not doubt, but I shall have the Concurrence of my politest Readers on this Head. As for the other Copy, it is only a short *Poetical Billet*, which our Author, it seems, could write as readily as many others do in plain Prose; but it proves that the Ladies can be no less warm in their Affections than their humble Servants, and that they are equally impatient, *on Absence*, how much soever they are capable of disguising their Passion, wherein it is confessed they have generally the Advantage of the Men. (2:29, introducing poems 25–26, "To my Love" and "To the Same")

3. INTRODUCTIONS TO THE OTHER FEMALE-AUTHORED ANONYMOUS LOVE POEMS

Saturday, June 17, 1732.
The following Copy of Verses was never before in Print, tho' wrote many Years ago. There are Instances enough of the Havock which *Love* makes among the Men, and we hardly know a Dabler in Poetry, or indeed a good Poet, who does not complain of the Cruelty of his Mistress. What I now present the Publick, is the tender Lamentation of a fair Lady, on being disappointed of suitable Returns to her Passion; and whether her's was sincere, or not, is submitted to the experienced Readers of either Sex. For my own Part, I do not doubt it; nor can I help wishing, therefore, as old as I am, that 'twas in my Power to administer Relief to so much Anguish in a Female Breast. (1:26, introducing poem 28, "Written at Midnight")

Wednesday, April 25, 1733.
SIR,
Since there are very few young Persons unmarried, of either Sex, that do not propose sometime or other to alter their Condition; and Marriage is a State that must make them happy or miserable for the Remainder of their Lives, it may be well worth while to consider what ought to be the first and chief Inducement to the entering upon it. I am fully sensible how the Generality of the World have thought of this Matter, by their Practice; and am no less appris'd of the direful Effects of it. I shall not scruple therefore to advance, that there never was, in common Life, a youthful Couple join'd together in Wedlock, who had not previously conceived a real Affection for each other, but dearly repented of it afterwards. From whence it will be easily inferr'd, that I reckon *Love* ought always to be the principal Ingredient, without which, let the Circumstances of the Parties be what they will, I am persuaded they are seldom better'd by Matrimony, how much soever outward Appearances may seem to favour, or promise such an Event.

There is, no doubt, a becoming Reservedness in the other Sex, and an habitual Modesty which makes it indecent, at least at first, to be as explicit on the Point, as Custom permits in ours; but when they come to be convinced that they are address'd upon honourable Terms, and with serious Views, those Restraints soon wear off, and give way to the Dictates of Nature, which are the same in both Parts of the Species, the great Author of it having, for the necessary Continuance of the Race, implanted an equal Propensity one towards the other. As the tender Fair therefore know how to signify their Inclinations when it is proper, and their humble Servants need not be at a Loss to discover them, I would recommend it to the Latter, before they proceed too far, to be no less assur'd, that they are *belov'd*, than that they *love*; in which Case, I dare promise a successful Match; and, in Justice to the Former, must declare, that I believe there are scarce any Instances to be met with, of their proving false where they once yielded their Hearts, without great Provocation, and a prior Breach of the reciprocal Bond, on the other Side.

But, instead of arguing on the Subject, I shall rather chuse to entertain the Reader with an Example of mutual Affection in two valuable Persons of my Acquaintance, which commenced whilst they were both very young. As the Gentleman had, after mature Deliberation, fixed his Thoughts on one that was in herself every way deserving, so he did not fail to meet with those Returns he expected; which last, I presume, will be readily allow'd me from the Specimen hereafter to be given. Those, that have experienced any thing of the *Passion*, cannot be surprized at the Occasional Uneasiness they will observe in the *Lovers*, and the good-natured Critick will excuse any Incorrectness in the Poetry, when he considers that, being of the familiar Sort, it was never intended to be made publick; and when he is further told, that it was casually preserved from the Flames, to which a great deal more from the same Pen was committed, in Compliance with the earnest Request of their Author, whose riper and more study'd Performances were so far from needing an Apology, that they excited Admiration.

The Lover in the Course of his Addresses, having once apprehended that his Charmer had shewn some Coldness towards him, could not long forbear discovering the Fears he entertained of that Kind, which, as soon as perceived, were effectually removed by the following Lines. (1:150–51, introducing poem 30, "Why pants my fondest tender Dove")

At another Time the Lady herself had conceived some Jealousy of him, as will appear from what she wrote on that Occasion, which is in a quite different Strain from the first; and wherein she blames him with downright Supineness and Neglect. (1:152, introducing poem 31, "Your kind Example cures me more")

But the Scene is now entirely changed again, and she seems to be all over in Rapture. (1:153, introducing poem 32, "I chide the Winds, and hate the Air")

What comes next, was a Reprimand she gave him for hinting, in Conversation, some good Things concerning another Lady, for whom it was reported, that he had a greater Kindness than she desired he should. (1:153, introducing poem 33, "On naming Mrs. * * * *")

But what must have given *Strephon* the strongest Assurance of his Mistress's most ardent Affection, are the subsequent Lines; with which therefore I shall conclude this Epistle, designed purely to amuse the Young and the Gay for the present, and to caution them for the future, in one of the most important Affairs of Life. (1:154, introducing poem 34, "When Oh! my Stars, when will ye join")

Saturday, March 30, 1734.
SIR,
Should you want to fill up a Paper at any Time, you may insert the following Lines which were hastily wrote by a Young Lady to her Lover, the first favourable Opportunity she had, after seeing him from her Chamber-Windows, where it was improper for her to seem to take Notice of him. I believe you will think it a Proof that the *Fair* are as capable of Heroism in Love, as the Men; and for my own Part I am very apt to think, notwithstanding the Raillery so plentifully bestowed on that Sex by ours, that they are generally much more constant too. (1:300, introducing poem 37, "My longing Bosom wish'd to throw")

Saturday, May 11, 1734.
What I shall give, for the Entertainment of this Day, came, if I mistake not, from a Gentleman to whom I am indebted for some of the most ingenious and valuable Performances that have at any Time appear'd in my Paper. Besides several fine Original Pieces of Poetry, that had long remain'd in Manuscript, on Subjects of Amusement, and which I take to have been handed to me thro' his Means, I have particularly observ'd that his Letters tended to promote Religion and Virtue, with a constant View to the General Good of the Island; and all of them were intirely free from *Prejudice* or *Party.* 'Tis to be hoped therefore I may be pardon'd for saying thus much concerning so worthy a Person, especially when I declare that nothing shall induce a further Discovery but Leave from the Author, which I do not expect to obtain.

SIR,   *Bridge-Town, May 9, 1734.*
Tho' some of your Correspondents have discover'd an honest and useful Spirit, as well as a good Genius, in several Letters lately inserted in the *Barbados-Gazette,* concerning the Authors of our Pub-

lick Misfortunes; yet I apprehend it is now highly proper to cultivate a good Understanding amongst one another, leaving Capital Offenders to be prosecuted and punished according to Law, without either Favour or Malice, both equally prejudicial to *Justice, which alone,* as Sir *Richard Steele* rightly says, *can prevail for any Duration of Time.* 'Tis to be hop'd, however, that such, as have done amiss in a lower Degree, will do so no more, and that such, as have been misled, will be less unwary for the future, whilst all others resolve to exercise their Talents, and exert their utmost Abilities, in the real Service of their Country. There is nothing, in my Opinion, that contributes more to publick or private Happiness than a benevolent Disposition, and which should on that Score, methinks, be encourag'd, as well as on Account of its being agreeable to the whole Tenour of the Christian Religion. For my own Part, I will not be asham'd to confess that I never could take Delight in reading the best Satyrical Writings that fell in my Way, but generally thought the Wit intirely destroy'd, by the Ill-Nature I met with in them; which I mention without alluding, in the least, to any Thing I have seen in your Papers, since they seem to aim more at the Crimes than the Persons, in all Cases but where it was necessary to point out the latter. 'Tis for this Reason, indeed, that I can by no Means be an Admirer of a late celebrated Performance, though I have perus'd some others of the Author's Works almost with Rapture. But it shocks me, I own, to observe a Gentleman, and a Scholar, endeavouring, contrary to his own Knowledge, to represent most of his Contemporaries of considerable Characters in the learned World, as mere *Dunces*; and at the same Time I equally blame these last, in giving too just Occasion for it, by having suffer'd their own Pens to run into the like Error: Nor can I doubt, but the Authors of such like Compositions, whatever Sensations may at first arise, will feel less Pleasure than Pain, from a serious Reflection thereon, towards the End of Life. The two following *Pieces* (to introduce which I was led to this Subject) are of a quite different Nature, and, tho' they were wrote many Years ago, have never yet, to my Knowledge, been in Print; but 'tis presum'd they will not be judg'd unworthy of it by your polite Readers, especially those that possess the Quality I have been recommending, for whose Amusement you have now Leave to publish them, by

Your humble Servant.

(1:321–22, introducing poem 38, "To Mr. -------- on his having resolved to write no more," and "The Answer. To the most excellent and most admirable Clio")

Saturday, August 17, 1734.

SIR,   *Barbados, Aug. 13, 1734.*
Boccalini, in his *Advices from Parnassus,* tells us, that the Academy
of the *Intronati* once took it in their Heads, contrary to their Original
Institution, to admit several Poetesses into their Society: That the
Academicks, being fired with the Wit and Beauty of the Ladies, not
only frequented their Company in great Numbers, but likewise pub-
lished every Day such Flights of Poetry as even as the Muses them-
selves were amazed at. But that, in a little Time, *Apollo* began to
smell a Rat, and commanded the chief of the *Intronati* forthwith to
put a Stop to this Practice. He told them, he was at last convinced,
that the fittest Poetry for Females was the *Needle and the Distaff;*
and in short, that the Exercise of Learning between them and the
Virtuosi is but like the Play of Dogs, which commonly ends in getting
upon one another's Backs. As the Poetry of the Ladies of this Island
is generally of the Kind recommended by *Apollo* himself, there can
be no Danger of the evil Consequences that were apprehended in
Parnassus. On the contrary, 'tis to be feared, that if the Female Wits
and Beauties of *Barbados* were never to have a *Game at Romps,* but
what should be set on Foot, and occasioned by such a Poetical Inter-
course as our Author relates, they must lead but melancholy Lives,
since, how capable soever my fair Countrywomen may be on their
Part, I doubt, there are but few of the other Sex that will ever *amaze
the Muses* with their Performances in that Way. Be this, however, as
it will, I now send you a Poetical Epistle wrote many Years ago (but
never yet in Print) by a young Lady in *London,* to a Gentleman of
her Acquaintance, who was then gone down into *Wales,* for a little
Retirement. The Images which are raised in the Letter do, I confess,
bring to my Remembrance several very agreeable Scenes I have my-
self known in a Country Retirement, in *Europe,* during my younger
Years, some whereof were spent there; and 'tis possible they may
have the same Effect on many others of your Readers. (1:372–73, in-
troducing poem 39, "To *Aberglasney*")

Wednesday, January 26, 1737.
SIR,
Since you have often entertain'd your Readers with agreeable
Pieces, from a Female Hand, I will venture to send you one which
was wrote by a Lady to whom I had the Honour of being known some
Years ago, and which I presume you will likewise think not unworthy
of a Place in your Paper. (2:183, introducing poem 41, "A Pastoral
Song")

Appendix B: Texts of other poems for comparison

1. FRANCIS ATTERBURY, "EPIGRAM WRITTEN BY OUR AUTHOR
ON A WHITE FAN BORROWED FROM MISS OSBORNE,
AFTERWARDS HIS WIFE"

Flavia the least and slightest toy
Can with resistless art employ:
This Fan in meaner hands would prove
An engine of small force in love;
Yet she with graceful air and mien,   5
Not to be told, or safely seen,
Directs its wanton motions so,
That it wounds more than Cupid's bow;
Gives coolness to the matchless dame,
To every other breast—a flame.   10

The Miscellaneous Works of Bishop Atterbury, ed. J. Nichols, 4 vols. (London: printed by and for the editor, 1789–90), 3:296. Nichols indicates that the poem was first published in March 1692 in the *Gentleman's Journal*; it was also printed, with minor variants, in James Greenwood, *The Virgin Muse* (London: J. Wyat and others, 1717; 2nd ed., 1722), 140, and in Giles Jacob, *An Historical Account of the Lives and Writings of our most considerable English Poets*, 2 vols. (London: E. Curll, 1720), 1:3.

2. ALEXANDER POPE, "WALLER: ON A FAN OF THE AUTHOR'S
DESIGN, IN WHICH WAS PAINTED THE STORY OF CEPHALUS AND
PROCRIS WITH THE MOTTO, *AURA VENI*"

Come, gentle Air! th' *Æolian* Shepherd said,
While *Procris* panted in the secret shade;

Come, gentle Air, the fairer *Delia* cries,
While at her feet her swain expiring lies.
Lo the glad gales o'er all her beauties stray,   5
Breathe on her lips, and in her bosom play!
In *Delia*'s hand this toy is fatal found,
Nor could that fabled dart more surely wound:
Both gifts destructive to the givers prove;
Alike both lovers fall by those they love.   10
Yet guiltless too this bright destroyer lives,
At random wounds, nor knows the wound she gives:
She views the story with attentive eyes,
And pities *Procris*, while her lover dies.

First printed in the *Spectator*, no. 527, 4 November 1712; the version above first appeared in the edition of Pope's *Works* in 1741. See *The Poems of Alexander Pope*, Twickenham Edition, 11 vols. (London: Methuen, 1938–68), *Minor Poems*, ed. Norman Ault and John Butt (1954), 6:45–47.

3. SAMUEL JONES, "TO LESBIA, *WITH A FAN*"

I.

Go Agent of Delight,
To th' Hands where all the Graces meet;
Beneath their Empire thou
Than Scepters wil't more awful show,
And all Things yielding find, or all subdue.   5

II.

Go when she needs thee most,
And tell her what of me thou know'st;
Oh! tell her, while she warms
The Fire Love kindles with her Charms,
All Intermission and all Art disarms.   10

III.

Then when she cooler grows,
Conjure her by the Calm she knows,

To do the like for me;
A gentle Breath of hers will be
More sovereign to my Soul than to her Body thee.   15

*Poetical Miscellanies on Several Occasions. By Samuel Jones,
Gent.* (London: A. Bettesworth and E. Curll, 1714), 47.

4. ANONYMOUS, "ON MISS P–N M–RT–N'S FAN"

Thrice happy toy, whose gales delight the fair,
Breath on her face, and wanton in her hair;
When next impatient of the noon-tide heats,
To some cool grot the lovely maid retreats;
When thy soft zephyrs ev'ry feature court,   5
Play on her neck, and in her bosom sport;
Bid her, when cool'd, by thy refreshing breeze,
Think how with heat I glow, and give me ease.

*A New Miscellany: Being a Collection of Pieces of Poetry, from
Bath, Tunbridge, Oxford, Epsom, and other Places* (London: T.
Warner, 1725), 63.

5. MARTHA FOWKE, *ON THE SAD THOUGHT OF PARTING*

Scarce can my Soul the killing Fear sustain,
    Of the sad Death its Joys must quickly die,
The Days and Nights of never-ceasing Pain,
    When absent from thy Life-inspiring Eye,
When smiling Hope which soft Relief bestows,   5
Will leave me to the Deluge of my Woes.

Methinks I feel like the lost lavish Heir,
    Who sees the last of his declining Store,
And ev'ry Morning wakes to new Despair,
    And starts at the sad Thought of being poor.   10
But ah! the Simile is far below
The noble Misery I undergoe.

To some new Scene the Bankrupt may remove,
   And court again the Favour of his Fate,
But all my Treasure is in tender Love,   15
   Spring of my Life, and my Soul's sole Estate,
Without thee I should languish on a Throne,
And, crowded by the World, be still alone.

Oh sweet Companion! finish'd to my Mind,
   Ev'ry Perfection in thy Person shines,   20
Wise as a God, as melting Mercy kind,
   Sweet in thy Looks, transporting in thy Lines.
Oh! Soul of Beauty, Nature wond'ring stands
At her great Work, and blesses her own Hands.

Happy for me if I had ne'er survey'd   25
   The fatal Treasurer of all her Charms,
Insensible this bosom might have laid,
   Dully contented in cold lawful Arms,
Nor dream'd, encharm'd by those dear Eyes of thine,
Of heav'nly Riches that can ne'er be mine.   30

The happy Villager contented seems,
   To all the fine Desires of Life unknown,
He unrepining drinks the cooling Streams,
   Talks to the Groves, nor knows he is alone.
But thou, alas! art Nectar to my Heart,   35
And I must sink in Death, whene'er we part.

Clio: or, A Secret History of the Life and Amours of the Late Celebrated Mrs. S——N——M (London: M. Cooper, 1752), 194–96; *Clio*, ed. Phyllis J. Guskin, 143–44.

Notes

Preface

1. The five surviving issues from the 1730s are described in the Introduction below; the others are listed by Jerome S. Handler in *A Guide to Source Materials for the Study of Barbados History, 1627–1834* (Carbondale and Edwardsville: Southern Illinois University Press; London and Amsterdam: Feffer & Simons, 1971), 116–17; and *Supplement to A Guide to Source Materials for the Study of Barbados History, 1627–1834* (Providence, RI: John Carter Brown Library and the Barbados Museum and Historical Society, 1991), 49.

2. *Caribbeana: Containing Letters and Dissertations, Together with Poetical Essays, on Various Subjects and Occasions; Chiefly wrote by several Hands in the West-Indies, and some of them to Gentlemen residing there* (T. Osborne, J. Clarke, S. Austin, G. Hawkins, R. Dodsley, and W. Lewis; repr. Millwood, NY: Kraus Reprint, 1978). Further references are given in the text by volume and page numbers in parentheses. Thirteen of the poems have been reprinted in *Caribbeana: An Anthology of English Literature of the West Indies, 1657–1777,* ed. Thomas W. Krise (Chicago and London: University of Chicago Press, 1999), 147–65. These are identified in the notes to the poems below.

3. Oxford and New York: Oxford University Press, 1989, 145–49. Lonsdale's *New Oxford Book of Eighteenth-Century Verse* first appeared in 1984 (Oxford and New York: Oxford University Press).

4. " 'Not Originally Intended for the Press': Martha Fowke Sansom's Poems in the *Barbados Gazette,*" *Eighteenth-Century Studies,* 34 (2000), 61–91; *Clio: The Autobiography of Martha Fowke Sansom (1689–1736)* (Newark, NJ: University of Delaware Press; London: Associated University Presses, 1997), 15, 166. In subsequent references this edition is cited as *Clio.* I am grateful to Phyllis Guskin for sending me typescripts both of her conference paper and of her article, and proofs of the latter.

Introduction

1. Howard S. Pactor, *Colonial British Caribbean Newspapers: A Bibliography and Directory* (New York and London: Greenwood Press, 1990), ix; Isaiah Thomas, *The History of Printing in America,* 2 vols. (Worcester, MA: Isaiah Thomas, Jun., 1810), 2:386; 2nd ed. (Albany, NY: Joel Munsell, 1874), 2:188. For a modern history of early American newspapers, see Charles E. Clark, *The Public Prints: The Newspaper in Anglo-American Culture, 1665–1740* (New York and Oxford: Oxford University Press, 1994).

2. "Some Notes on Early Printing Presses and Newspapers in Barbados," *Journal of the Barbados Museum and Historical Society*, 26:1 (November 1958), 19–33 (p. 21).

3. London: W. Boreham, 1718. The fullest account of Keimer's life is by C. Lennart Carlson, "Samuel Keimer: A Study in the Transit of English Culture to Colonial Pennsylvania," *Pennsylvania Magazine of History and Biography*, 61 (1937), 357–86, extending and supplementing Stephen Bloore, "Samuel Keimer: A Footnote to the Life of Franklin," *Pennsylvania Magazine of History and Biography*, 54 (1930), 255–87.

4. See Elizabeth Christine Cook, *Literary Influences in Colonial Newspapers 1704–1750* (New York and London: Columbia University Press, 1912), 59–61.

5. See Charles E. Clark and Charles Wetherell, "The Measure of Maturity: The *Pennsylvania Gazette*, 1728–1765," *William and Mary Quarterly*, 3d series, 46 (1989), 279–303; and Charles E. Clark, *The Public Prints*, 171–76.

6. *The Autobiography of Benjamin Franklin*, ed. Leonard W. Labaree, Ralph L. Ketcham, Helen C. Boatfield, and Helene H. Fineman (New Haven and London: Yale University Press, 1964), 126.

7. *The Autobiography of Benjamin Franklin*, 126; *History of Printing in America*, 2:48 (1810 ed.), 1:241 (1874 ed.).

8. The latest known copy is dated 16 March 1797. See Handler, *Supplement to A Guide to Source Materials for the Study of Barbados History*, 49.

9. Burney 289b; the reference in Handler's *Supplement* is incorrect. Two pages were probably printed on each side of a folio sheet. See Clark, *The Public Prints*, 7–8.

10. *History of Printing in America*, 2:386 (1810 ed.), 2:188 (1874 ed.); Shilstone, "Early Printing Presses and Newspapers in Barbados," 22.

11. The Prefaces are dated 17 December 1740, and 26 March 1741 (1:x, 2:xvi). Keimer died in Barbados on 20 August 1742 (Carlson, 386; Shilstone, 22).

12. "Not Originally Intended for the Press," 88, n. 15.

13. No issues at all are included after 8 October until 13 December 1735; after 22 May until 4 August 1736; after 18 August until 25 December 1736; after 26 January until 30 April 1737; or after 21 April until 15 September 1738.

14. Miscellanies were an important channel of publication for poetry at this period. Arthur E. Case identifies the great majority of those extant in *A Bibliography of English Poetical Miscellanies 1521–1750* (Oxford: Oxford University Press for the Bibliographical Society, 1935).

15. These are poems 27, 29, and 40. See the notes on poems 29 and 40 below.

16. *Calendar of State Papers, Colonial Series, America and the West Indies, 1726–1727*, ed. Cecil Headlam (London: HMSO, 1936), 135–36, 221–22; *Gentleman's Magazine*, July 1734, 4:391. For an account of Blenman's work as Judge of the Vice-Admiralty Court, see Richard Pares, "Barbados History from the Records of the Prize Courts," *Journal of the Barbados Museum and Historical Society*, 6:3 (May 1939), 117–28. A sign of Blenman's standing by 1740 is that it was to him that John Oldmixon dedicated the second edition of his history, *The British Empire in America*, 2 vols. (London: J. Brotherton and others, 1741).

17. Publications known to be by Blenman are: *A Letter to the Reverend Mr. Brydges, Rector of Croscombe in Somersetshire. [. . .] being a Vindication of the Dissenters* (London: John Clark, 1715); *The Mug Vindicated: To which is*

prefix'd, An account of the rise, progress, and constitution, of those loyal societies (London: S. Popping, 1717); *Remarks on the Trial of John Peter Zenger* (London: J. Roberts, 1738); and *Remarks on Several Acts of Parliament Relating More especially to the Colonies Abroad* (London: T. Cooper, 1742; repr. New York: Arno Press, 1972). Two letters by Blenman are printed in *The Barbadoes Packet* (London: S. Popping, 1720), and he also edited *A Letter from a Gentleman at Barbados to his Friend now in London, concerning the Administration of the late Governor B-----g,* of which he was the addressee (London: J. Roberts, 1740). See also the discussion on pp. 23–27 above. The British Library catalogue is mistaken in distinguishing between an elder Blenman, author of *A Letter to the Reverend Mr. Brydges* and *The Mug Vindicated,* and a younger Blenman, author of the other titles under the same name.

18. "Not Originally Intended for the Press," 67. Asterisks or dashes are often used to conceal or part-reveal identities in writing of the period. Though their number is not always an accurate guide to the number of letters in the name to which they refer (where this can be determined), it seems almost certain that they do so here.

19. "*To Philomela. Occasioned by her* Poem *on* the death of her Husband," and "*To the* Author *of the foregoing* Verses," in *The Miscellaneous Works in Prose and Verse of Mrs. Elizabeth Rowe,* 2 vols. (London: R. Hett and R. Dodsley, 1739), 1:116–17. In the *Caribbeana* versions, which feature minor variants in punctuation and italicization, the title of the first poem continues: "and particularly the two last Lines of it, *viz.*

> *That sacred Passion I to thee confine,*
> *My spotless Faith shall be for ever thine."*

The title of Rowe's poem as printed in *Caribbeana* is quite different: "To Mr. * * * * * *, at *Tom's* Coffee-House, in *Devereux-Court,* near the *Temple, London.*" Rowe lived in seclusion after her husband died in 1715; the poem referred to by her unwelcome suitor, "On the Death of Mr. Thomas Rowe," was first published on 13 July 1717 in *Poems on Several Occasions,* a miscellany probably edited by Pope who also contributed to it (London: Bernard Lintot). This date is consistent with the interval of "near seventeen Years" mentioned in *Caribbeana.*

20. For biographical details on Rowe, see Henry F. Stecher, *Elizabeth Singer Rowe: A Study in Eighteenth-Century English Pietism* (Bern: Herbert Lang; Frankfurt-am-Main: Peter Lang, 1973). Blenman's *Letter to the Reverend Mr. Brydges* indicates both that he was a Dissenter and that he came from Somerset; the latter fact is confirmed by the family tree in James C. Brandow (comp.), *Genealogies of Barbados Families* (Baltimore, MD: Genealogical Publishing, 1983), 177–79.

21. See Philip H. Highfill, Jr., Kalman A. Burnim, and Edward A. Langhans, *A Biographical Dictionary of Actors, Actresses, Musicians, Dancers, Managers, and Other Stage Personnel in London, 1660–1800,* 16 vols. (Carbondale and Edwardsville: Southern Illinois University Press, 1973–93), 8:283–85.

22. See Robert D. Horn, *Marlborough: A Survey. Panegyrics, Satires, and Biographical Writings, 1688–1788* (New York and London: Garland, 1975), 389–91. A version of the poem is given in Thomas Lediard, *The Life of John, Duke*

of Marlborough, 3 vols. (London: J. Wilcox, 1736), 3:297–98, from which Sir Winston Churchill, attributing the poem to Addison, quotes the first 12 lines in *Marlborough: His Life and Times,* 4 vols. (London: George Harrap, 1933–38), 4:577.

23. *Remarks on Zenger's tryal, taken out of the Barbados Gazette's; for the benefit of the students in law, and others in North America* (New York: 1770), cited by Handler, *Guide to Source Materials for the Study of Barbados History,* 42.

24. The quotation is from one of the items in the Appendix to *Caribbeana,* a report of a judicial commission of which Blenman was a member; it is on p. 44, with a footnote giving the *Caribbeana* page reference (2:353). The advertisement is on the last page (sig. R3ᵛ), and the British Library copy, shelfmark 8155.b.32, has the manuscript inscription "by Jonathan Blenman, Esq" on its title page. *A Letter from a Gentleman at Barbados* indicates that Blenman had left Barbados "a few Months before Mr. B---g's Arrival" (Preface, sig. a2ᵛ), which is given as 15 December 1739 (p. 3).

25. "Not Originally Intended for the Press," 88, n. 16; H. R. Plomer, G. H. Bushnell, and E. R. McC. Dix, *A Dictionary of the Printers and Booksellers who were at work in England, Scotland, and Ireland from 1726 to 1775* (Oxford: Oxford University Press for the Bibliographical Society, 1932).

26. Sig. a2ᵛ.

27. Joseph Foster, *Register of Admissions to Gray's Inn, 1521–1889* (London: Hansard Publishing Union, 1889), 375; Joseph Foster, *Alumni Oxonienses: The Members of the University of Oxford, 1715–1886,* 4 vols. (Oxford and London: James Parker, 1891), 1:223. The date of Timothy Blenman's matriculation was 17 December 1741, "aged 16."

28. *Register of Admissions to the Honourable Society of the Middle Temple from the Fifteenth Century to the Year 1944,* comp. H. A. C. Sturgess (London: Butterworth, 1949). The date of Blenman's own admission was 26 June 1710, and he was called to the Bar on 20 April 1716. Blenman's *Remarks on Several Acts of Parliament* includes a letter by him dated 11 June 1742, indicating that he was still in London at that date (78).

29. "Not Originally Intended for the Press," 65.

30. The dash in line 24 of "The Absent" could refer either to the lover or the poet. If it refers to the lover, it is curious that, as in poem 16, the poet also refers to him by his usual pseudonym, Damon, elsewhere in the same poem.

31. "Not Originally Intended for the Press," 67–68. Fowke died on 17 February 1736. The relevant phrase in the Preface concerning dating is: "then living here (since deceased)" (1:ix). Guskin reads this as meaning that the writer was alive at the time the poems were published in the *Gazette,* from 1731 to early 1736; but the word "then" seems more likely to refer to the date of their composition, suggesting that she died at some time between the period in which she wrote the poems, in 1720–21, and 1740, the date given at the end of the first preface.

32. In *Clio,* Fowke says she was writing verse when she was "about nine or ten Years old" (66); her epitaph remarks that she was composing poetry "from the age of sixteen." Her memorial in St Martin's, now the cathedral church of the city of Leicester, was covered by a new floor in 1865. The inscription, printed in the *Gentleman's Magazine* in 1781 (51:22), is quoted by Guskin (*Clio,* 39); it

appears with minor variations in John Nichols, *The History and Antiquities of the County of Leicester*, 4 vols. (London: Nichols and Bentley, 1795–1815; repr. Menston, Yorks.: Scolar Press, 1971), 1.2, *Town of Leicester and Indexes*, 597.

33. *Clio*, 9. The respective references are as follows: *Delights for the Ingenious: or, a Monthly Entertainment for the Curious of Both Sexes*, ed. John Tipper (London: J. Roberts, 1711), 129–31; Giles Jacob, *An Historical Account of the Lives and Writings of our Most Considerable English Poets* (London: E. Curll, 1720; vol. 2 of *The Poetical Register*, 1719), 326, and *Human Happiness* (London: T. Jauncy and J. Roberts, 1721), 43–44; *The Epistles of Clio and Strephon, being a Collection of Letters that passed between an English Lady, and an English Gentleman in France* (London: J. Hooke, F. Gyles, and W. Boreham, 1720); *A New Miscellany of Original Poems, Translations and Imitations*, ed. Antony Hammond (London: T. Jauncy, 1720); and *Miscellaneous Poems and Translations*, ed. Richard Savage (London: Samuel Chapman, 1726).

34. *Clio*, 81–82; *Memoirs of a Certain Island Adjacent to the Kingdom of Utopia*, 2 vols. (London: Booksellers of London and Westminster, 1725–26; vol. 1 repr. New York and London: Garland, 1972), 1:43–49, 183–86. Guskin reprints some passages from Haywood's book in *Clio*, and, on pp. 28–31, discusses the relationship between the two writers.

35. Fowke refers to herself as "Miss *Patty*" in *Clio*, 65; as Guskin points out (154), this was a common nickname for Martha.

36. "Not Originally Intended for the Press," 74–77.

37. *Calendar of State Papers, Colonial Series, America and the West Indies, January, 1719 to February, 1720*, ed. Cecil Headlam (London: HMSO, 1933), 267; *March, 1720 to December, 1721*, pp. 15–17, 18. The *Journal of the Commissioners for Trade and Plantations from November 1718 to December 1722* (London: HMSO, 1925) summarizes the evidence given by Blenman and Hope (155–56). The struggle against Lowther is recorded in Oldmixon, *The British Empire in America*, 2:66–71; in John Poyer, *The History of Barbados* (London: J. Mawman, 1808), 216–20; and in Sir Robert H. Schomburgk, *The History of Barbados* (London: Longman, Brown, Green and Longmans, 1848), 314–17.

38. *The Barbadoes Packet; Containing Several Original Papers: giving an Account of the Most Material Transactions that have lately happened in a certain Part of the West-Indies* (S. Popping). The pamphlet includes two letters from Blenman and a copy of the document committing him for trial.

39. In *The South Sea Bubble* (London: Cresset Press, 1960), John Carswell dates the start of "nationwide financial panic" from 26 September (184).

40. London: Published for the Author, 1720, p. 156.

41. *Calendar of State Papers, Colonial Series, America and the West Indies, March, 1720 to December, 1721*, p. 213. The *Journal of the Commissioners for Trade and Plantations from November 1718 to December 1722* indicates that Lowther left Barbados on 30 June 1720 (346).

42. Sig. A3ᵛ, italics reversed.

43. "Not Originally Intended for the Press," 75 and 90 n. 40; Schomburgk, *History of Barbados*, 316, citing *Caribbeana*, 1:394.

44. *Clio*, 131; "Not Originally Intended for the Press," 88, n. 22.

45. *Barbados Records: Baptisms 1637–1800*, comp. and ed. Joanne McCree Sanders (Baltimore, MD: Genealogical Publishing, 1982), 66; *Calendar of State*

Papers [. . .] 1722–1723, p. 242; *Calendar of State Papers [. . .] March, 1720 to December, 1721*, p. 346. If Blenman was in London in 1722, he would have been away for the baptism of his son as he had been for that of his daughter Mary on 5 June 1720 (Sanders, 64). The Blenmans' next child, Timothy, was born on 5 March 1724, and baptized on 2 April (73).

46. *Barbados Records: Baptisms 1637–1800*, p. 58. Nicholas Hope's birthdate is recorded in the same source as 9 October 1693 (33).

47. "Not Originally Intended for the Press," 66–67. Of the name Clio, a letter about the Savage miscellany in the *British Journal* of 24 September 1726 claims: "it has of late been so abus'd and scandaliz'd, that I am inform'd she has lately chang'd it for that of *Mira*" (210:2). For information about Hill and his circle, see Dorothy Brewster, *Aaron Hill: Poet, Dramatist, Projector* (New York: Columbia University Press, 1913).

48. See Brewster, 56–59 and 101–4; and Highfill, Burnim, and Langhans, *Biographical Dictionary*, 7:298–299.

49. See Ralph M. Williams, *Poet, Painter, and Parson: The Life of John Dyer* (New York: Bookman Associates, 1956), 60–2, 80. Guskin attributes the poem to Hill partly on the basis of its reference to the writer and Clio attending a play, since Hill and Fowke seem to have first met at the theatre ("Not Originally Intended for the Press," 66 and 88 n. 22). However, Dyer would certainly also have been a theatregoer.

50. "Not Originally Intended for the Press," 67; *Clio*, 25, 37, 167.

51. "Not Originally Intended for the Press," 67.

52. In his edition of the poem, *Grongar Hill: By John Dyer* (Baltimore, MD: Johns Hopkins University Press, 1941), Richard C. Boys considers the different states of the poem. These range from early manuscript fragments in heroic couplets, through the Pindaric version in *Miscellaneous Poems and Translations*, ed. Savage, to the final version in tetrameter couplets, not published till 1761 but anticipated twice in 1726, first incompletely, in *A New Miscellany: Being a Collection of Pieces of Poetry, from Bath, Tunbridge, Oxford, Epsom, and other Places*, ed. T. Warner (London: T. Warner), then by a complete version in *Miscellaneous Poems, by Several Hands*, ed. D. Lewis (London: J. Watts). Since "To Aberglasney" responds to "Grongar Hill," it is likely to have been written in the same verse form as that of the latter two versions, both first published in 1726; since they appear to postdate the version in the Savage miscellany, it was probably written later in the same year.

53. Approximate dates for some of Dyer's movements in the 1720s between London and Wales are given by Ralph M. Williams in *Poet, Painter, and Parson*, 46, 48–49, 51, 63, 67–68, 71–76; for the likelihood that Fowke was required by her husband to retire from the Hill circle, see 75–76. Guskin discusses Fowke's marriage and her withdrawal from the literary scene in *Clio*, 37–38.

54. "Not Originally Intended for the Press," 71–72 (p. 72).

55. "Not Originally Intended for the Press," 68–69.

56. Perhaps the most surprising example is Fowke's reference to her father's murder in *The Epistles of Clio and Strephon*, a work which is in other ways highly artificial. See Martha Fowke and William Bond, *The Epistles of Clio and Strephon*, 85, reproduced in facsimile in John Porter, *A Critical Essay, Containing some Remarks upon the Nature of Epistolary and Elegiac Poetry* (New York: Garland, 1971). Fowke also refers to key events of her life in

"To Mr. Savage, on telling me his Misfortunes," a complimentary poem first published in Savage's miscellany (300–303).

57. "Not Originally Intended for the Press," 89 n. 34, 90 n. 46. Guskin says that the marriage took place in 1720 ("Not Originally Intended for the Press," 63).

58. Fowke mentions her brother pressing her to marry Sansom in *Clio*, 129. He had earlier tried to persuade her to marry another man (89–90).

POEMS BY THE ANONYMOUS LADY

1. On Reading Dr. Donne's Poems. 1:183–84; Wednesday, 18 July 1733. Reprinted by Robert C. Fox, "Donne in the British West Indies," *History of Ideas News Letter*, 5 (1960), 77–80; and by A. J. Smith, ed., *John Donne: The Critical Heritage* (London and Boston: Routledge and Kegan Paul, 1975), 197–99.

Cowley: Abraham Cowley (1618–1667), influenced by Donne and author of *The Mistress* (1647), a collection of love poems noted both for their wit and lack of passion.

Waller: Edmund Waller (1606–1687), famous for his love lyrics.

Lansdown: George Granville, first Baron Lansdowne (1667–1735), whose *Poems on Several Occasions* (1712) contains some rather conventional love poems, and to whom Pope dedicated *Windsor Forest* (1713).

Congreve: William Congreve (1670–1729) wrote both prose narratives and verse, including love poems, though he is better known as a dramatist.

Addison: Joseph Addison (1672–1719) is now remembered chiefly for his prose, especially his contributions to *The Tatler* and *Spectator,* but was also a poet and dramatist.

Prior: Matthew Prior (1664–1721), whose *Poems on Several Occasions* (1718) includes some amatory verse.

Numbers: literally, metrical feet; more broadly, versification.

wanted: in these poems "want" usually has the older sense of "lack": "to be destitute of, or deficient in" (*OED*).

Flame: love, passion; a common Restoration and earlier eighteenth-century usage deriving from the French. "Tenderness" probably also harks back to French, as in the famous Map of Tenderness in Madeleine de Scudéry's novel *Clélie* (1654–1660).

Fondling: refers to her heart, mentioned in the previous line.

Art: "studied conduct or action"; "cunning, artfulness" (*OED*); the way in which the poem varies the sense of this word is discussed on p. 87.

In Absence all my Thoughts survey'd: the full stop ending this line in *Caribbeana* has been emended to a comma.

2. To * * * * * * * * * ["Believe me; but my Actions speak"]. 1:248; Wednesday, 28 November 1733. Reprinted in *Caribbeana*, ed. Krise, 151.

3. To the Same ["Lost to my longing Arms and Eyes"]. 1:248–49; Wednesday, 28 November 1733. Reprinted in Krise, 151–52.

one short Year: one of the few indications of time in the series.

4. To the Same. A Pastoral. 1:249–50; Wednesday, 28 November 1733. Reprinted in Krise, 152–53.

Fondness: "affectionateness, tenderness" (*OED*); the context does not suggest the older sense of "foolishness," though it was still current.

Lyre: traditional symbol for lyric verse, which in ancient times was sung to musical accompaniment.

The Words of Antony: John Dryden, *All For Love: or, The World Well Lost*, 2.285–88. The poet has freely adapted Dryden's lines, reducing the original four to three. First performed in 1677, the play returned to favor with a lavish and successful production at Drury Lane in December 1718 which the poet may well have attended.

approve: to bear out or make proof of, rather than the more modern sense of confirming something or regarding it favorably, as in line 31 below and in line 6 of poem 2.

Grotto, Flowers, Linnets, Swain: all parts of the convention of pastoral to which the poem refers.

my Darling Crook, my tuneful Reed: the shepherdess's crook, and the reed-pipe—traditionally played by the shepherd rather than by his beloved.

5. Occasioned by his Illness. 1:264–65; Wednesday, 7 February 1734. Reprinted in Krise, 153–54.

feels, for thee: not necessarily an error of agreement between plural subject and singular verb form, if "Soul and Body" is understood as a singular subject. See also poem 15, line 30, and the note to poem 9, below.

join: at this period the diphthong "oi" would have been pronounced to rhyme with "mine."

I'll catch thy Soul: probably an echo of the death of Dido in Virgil's *Aeneid*, Book 4 (lines 982–83 in Dryden's translation). See further the discussion on pp. 107–8.

Cordials: medicines which invigorate the heart.

wing: put wings upon, speed up.

6. His Picture. 1:266; Wednesday, 7 February 1734.

Gentle Love: addressing Cupid, God of Love.

Pencil: paintbrush; the line means "Let your arrow be your brush."

killing: "overpoweringly beautiful or attractive" (*OED*).

discover: "reveal, show" (*OED*).

Bacchus: God of Wine.

thy own fond Mother: Venus, mother of Cupid.

Damon: a name often used for a male lover in pastoral poetry; applied by the anonymous lady to her addressee.

painted in: ambiguous—the phrase could mean "has painted pictures in," or "has confined by painting."

7. Written on one of his Letters. 1:266–67; Wednesday, 7 February 1734.

Forms: customary social and/or moral obligations.

8. On a Fan Presented. 1:267–68; Wednesday, 7 February 1734. Fans, much in vogue in the early eighteenth century, were the subject of a number of humorous poems and essays, the latter especially in *The Spectator*. See the discussion on pp. 92–93 and the fan poems in appendix B.

Trojan, Golden Fleece: the reference is clearly to Jason, who led the Argonauts on an expedition to capture the Golden Fleece but who did not hail from Troy. There are various ways of explaining the apparent solecism. First, it may derive from longstanding association of the Argonaut legend and that of Troy, pointed out by Virginia Knight in *The Renewal of Epic: Responses to Homer in the Argonautica of Apollonius* (Leiden, New York and Köln: E. J. Brill, 1995), passim, and by Jean Seznec in *The Survival of the Pagan Gods: The Mythological Tradition and its Place in Renaissance Humanism and Art*, trans. Barbara F. Sessions (Princeton: Princeton University Press, 1953; repr. 1972), 32. Second, in light not only of Jason's betrayal of Medea, but Aeneas's of Dido, the word "Trojan" may have been chosen for its undertone of faithlessness. Third, the poet is probably playing on the eighteenth-century slang sense, meaning a dissolute roisterer, as part of her parody of mock-epic. The word is used in this sense by Gay in *The Fan*, 2:104, and annotated accordingly in *John Gay: Poetry and Prose*, ed. Vinton A. Dearing and Charles E. Beckwith, 2 vols. (Oxford: Clarendon Press, 1974), 2:504. I am grateful to Gill Spraggs, Martha Davis, and Virginia Knight for their help with the classical part of this gloss.

Machine: a device or contrivance.

Magic Wood: Gill Spraggs has suggested to me that this may refer to the Dodonian oak, the oracular oak of Zeus, which had the power of speech and a part of which Athena had fitted to the prow of the ship Argo.

the Poet: this may be a generic term, referring to Apollonius of Rhodes and probably also Ovid, whose *Metamorphoses* contain many examples of the natural world giving voice. I am again indebted to Gill Spraggs for this suggestion.

Ivory: in contrast to the fan described by Gay, the sticks of this one are made of ivory.

Modish: fashionable; the choice of word is mildly satirical.

Silver Studs: used to fasten the fan together.

Colemar: mentioned as a maker of fans in *The Spectator* (No. 328, 17 March 1712); *OED* cites examples from 1727 and 1729.

9. To Mr. * * * * * * ["Oh! what retains thee now, what new Design"]. 1:276–77; Saturday, 2 March 1734.

Does not the Winds its ardent Sighings bear: "Winds" may be a misprint for "Wind", as the verb form and the pronoun "its" require a singular subject. However, there are technical errors of grammatical agreement between subject and verb both in poems assigned to the anonymous lady and in others contained in this edition, including the one by Clio. Although some older forms of English used the *-es* inflection for plural verbs, this was treated as a grammatical error as early as Shakespeare's Second Folio, printed in 1632. See Charles Barber, *Early Modern English* (London: André Deutsch, 1976), 244.

10. The Appeal. 1:277–78; Saturday, 2 March 1734.

Love: Cupid, God of Love.

Apollo: in his capacity as patron of poetry and leader of the Muses.

11. The Complaint. 1:278; Saturday, 2 March 1734.

the Hours: in classical mythology, female divinities presiding over the change of the seasons.

Time: Father Time, marked by his "silver shining Hair" (9).

12. The Absent. 1:278–79; Saturday, 2 March 1734.

Interest: "regard to one's own profit or advantage" (*OED*).

still: always (a common sense of the word at this period).

whilom call'd a Wit: "whilom" means "formerly"; these lines are evidence that the writer was already known in society for her work.

South-Sea: huge financial losses, resulting in ruin for many, followed the bursting of the South Sea Bubble in 1720; the allusion helps date both poem and love affair.

————: the dash is ambiguous; syntactically, it could refer either to addressee or poet.

13. Song ["While my Eyes are fondly speaking"]. 1:279–80; Saturday, 2 March 1734.

14. The Protestation. 1:280; Saturday, 2 March 1734.

brilliant: this idiosyncratic use of the word as a verb is not recorded by *OED* before 1752, when it is used to refer to the cutting of diamonds.

The dying Sappho lovely Phaon sung: according to a story which probably arose in the fourth century B.C.E., the poet Sappho fell in love with the ferryman Phaon and committed suicide by leaping from a cliff when he rejected her. In the eighteenth century, the story was best known from the *Heroides*, verse letters by the Roman poet Ovid (43 B.C.E.—17 C.E.), the fifteenth of which, "Sappho to Phaon," was often translated and imitated. For example, Alexander Pope's "Sapho to Phaon" was included in a translation of the *Heroides* first published in 1712. See *The Poems of Alexander Pope*, Twickenham Edition, 11 vols. (London: Methuen; New Haven: Yale University Press, 1938–68), *Pastoral Poetry and An Essay on Criticism*, ed. E. Audra and Aubrey Williams (1961), 1:392. Further references to poems by Pope are to this edition and are given in parentheses after the reference.

15. To Damon ["Go, faithful Paper, to my Love impart"]. 1:291–92; Wednesday, 20 March 1734. Reprinted in Krise, 154–56.

Venus: Goddess of Love, often accompanied by doves.

Damask Rose: species of rose supposed to have been originally brought from Damascus.

Tuby-Rose: a tuberose, *Polianthes tuberosa*; the flower is gardenia-scented and waxy white in color.

John-quill: jonquil, "a species of Narcissus [. . .] the rush-leaved Daffodil" (*OED*).

the God of Love [. . .] his Mother's Charms: Cupid, whose mother was Venus.

The Soul and Body hastens: as in poem 5, line 3, not necessarily an error of agreement if "Soul and Body" is understood as a singular subject.

His who warm'd to Life the jolly Maid: Pygmalion, a legendary king of Cyprus, fell in love with a statue of Venus—which, according to a version of the story in Ovid, he had himself carved out of ivory. In response to his prayer that he might have a wife as beautiful, Venus caused the statue to come to life; she was called Galatea. Dryden's translation of the story appeared in his *Fables Ancient and Modern* in 1700 and was included in the collaborative translation *Ovid's Metamorphoses in Fifteen Books* (London: Jacob Tonson, 1717). "Jolly" here means "pretty."

16. To the Same ["While to thy dear lov'd Arms I press"]. 1:292–93; Wednesday, 20 March 1734.

God of Verse: Apollo.

17. To the Same ["Let the God of Passion hear me"]. 1:293–94; Wednesday, 20 March 1734. Reprinted in Krise, 156.

God of Passion: Cupid, but probably emphasizing his earlier representation as Eros; a different figure from the "Train of Cupids" (4) familiar from Renaissance painting.

Fondling: her soul, mentioned in line 10; "my Soul" (15) refers to her lover whom she is addressing. Compare "On Reading Dr. Donne's Poems," line 37.

shock: "to damage or weaken by impact or collision" (*OED*).

18. To the Same ["Tho', blind with Love, I well perceive"]. 1:294–95; Wednesday, 20 March 1734.

Cynthia, Phoebus: names for the moon-goddess, Diana, and for the sun-god, Apollo.

Strings: nerves or muscular fibers.

beat: "to strive against contrary winds or currents at sea" (*OED*); this verb introduces the nautical metaphor of the next two lines.

19. On being charged with Writing incorrectly. 1:314–15; Saturday, 20 April 1734. Reprinted in the *Gentleman's Magazine* (June 1734), 4:327; in *Eighteenth-Century Women Poets*, ed. Lonsdale, 146–47; and in Krise, 157–58.

Hill of Fame: irreverent reference to Parnassus, sacred to Apollo and the Muses.

Genius: "characteristic disposition; inclination; bent, turn or temper of mind" (*OED*); the sense "native intellectual power of an exalted type" is later.

Rules: neoclassical conventions governing artistic creation.

Busby: Dr Richard Busby (1606–1695), notorious for severe discipline, had been a headmaster of Westminster School.

tuneful Sisters: the Muses, companions of Apollo and goddesses of creative inspiration in poetry, song and the other arts.

Silver Streams: springs presided over by the Muses which had the power to give inspiration: Aganippe and Hippocrene on Mount Helicon, and the Castalian spring on Mount Parnassus.

Dennis: John Dennis (1657–1734), though also a poet and dramatist, was the leading literary critic in England for at least twenty years from the early 1690s. He became notorious for rigor and bile after his attack on Pope's *Essay on Criticism* (1711).

20. Untitled ["To my Breast thy Verse applying"]. 1:336–37; Saturday, 1 June 1734. Reprinted in Krise, 158–60. The congruence of epigraph with poem suggests that it was written by the poet herself.

I would turn into a Tree: allusion to the myth of Daphne, who, pursued by Apollo, prayed to her father to save her and was turned into a laurel tree.

If he with his Stars descended: in his role as sun-god, Apollo was sometimes represented as driving his chariot across the Zodiac.

Which with meaner Hearts agree: error of agreement between subject ("Which," referring to "Every little Art") and verb. The plural verb form is required by the rhyme.

Flowing in my Verse to Thee: the comma ending this line in *Caribbeana* has been emended to a full stop.

21. A Letter to my Love.——All alone, past 12, in the Dumps. 1:360–62; Saturday, 29 June 1734. Reprinted in the *London Magazine* (November 1734), 3:600–601; the *European Magazine* (November 1788), 14:377–78; *Eighteenth-Century Women Poets*, ed. Lonsdale, 147–48; and Krise, 160–61. As with poem 20, and for the same reason, it is probable that the epigraph was written by the poet herself.

Dumps: a colloquial word which would have been thought indecorous in serious verse of the period.

Spleen: depression or melancholy.

zest: "to add a relish to" (*OED*); this early metaphorical use of the word may account for its italicization.

As if it was: *Caribbeana* reads "I" for "it," clearly a misprint.

shaded: sheltered. According to Phyllis Guskin, to whom I owe this gloss, the word is still used with such a meaning in Radnorshire.

tempest: rage or storm; *OED* records various examples of the use of the word in this sense as an intransitive verb.

want: "to feel the loss of, to miss" (*OED*).

Shadow: ghost, as in "Aerial Breast" two lines later.

22. Occasion'd by some Lines of his. 1:366–68; Wednesday, 24 July 1734. Reprinted in Krise, 161–63.

Genius: "natural ability or capacity" (*OED*).

chose: have chosen; "chose," rather than the modern past participle "chosen," was in common use at the period.

downy Feet: a delightful, witty pun on metrical feet.

great God of soft Desire: Cupid, whose "Dart," or arrow, is mentioned in line 18.

Strain: poetic song; verse.

complain: to express suffering, especially as a result of love.

Parnassus [. . .] Busby: the poet is attacking what she styles as the drudgery and pedantry of a traditional classical education, as she also does in poem 19.

You reach'd, so soon, the Place: "you reached the goal of success as a poet."

'Twas a Mistress tun'd thy Lyre: witty and mischievous play on the word "mistress"—both a female lover and a female mentor in poetry.

odious Rules: this phrase, and stanza, again echo poem 19.

Where Love, and lovely Nature, shines: not necessarily an error of agreement, if the subject is being treated as singular. The singular verb form is also required by the rhyme.

23. To Damon ["In vain, oh! much in vain, for Rest I seek"]. 2:6–7; Saturday, 9 November 1734. Reprinted in Krise, 163–64.

Reeds that do the Herdlings call: probably shepherds' pipes, as in pastoral poetry; *Herdlings* is not recorded in *OED*, but presumably means lambs.

Piece: the being created by Nature, i.e., the poet's lover.

Which warms the Form I love, and is my Friend: the subject of the singular verbs "warms" and "is" is "Soul," not "Beauties."

and Death be wondrous late: the expression is elliptical, but the poet is wishing that her lover will live for a long time.

right divine: guess or interpret correctly. I owe this gloss to Phyllis Guskin.

24. To my Love. Wrote in Tears ["Dearest Creature of thy Kind"]. 2:7; Saturday, 9 November 1734. Reprinted in Krise, 164–65.

Leander's Arms: Leander had to swim the Hellespont, the stretch of sea between modern Greece and Turkey now known as the Strait of Dardanelles, to meet his lover Hero. The allusion is ominous, because Leander drowned and Hero threw herself into the sea in despair; it is also unusual, because the poet has given herself the male role.

Kind: nature, presumably as a human, physical being; the sense of the word meaning "gender" is not recorded in *OED* after 1590.

25. To my Love ["When in my fond Embraces fast confin'd"]. 2:29–30; Saturday, 1 March 1735. Reprinted in *Eighteenth-Century Women Poets*, ed. Lonsdale, 148–49.

Adieu: the word implies a parting for a long time, perhaps for ever.

meet, with artful Tenderness: see Keimer's introductory remarks on the poem in appendix A, p. 121.

dull: insensible, obtuse; perhaps even foolish.

26. To the Same ["Time's Wings are lost now thy dear Eyes are gone"]. 2:30–31; Saturday, 1 March 1735.

Droops with my Cares: error of agreement between subject and verb, probably because "Time" is being understood for "Time's Wings" as a singular subject.

Where the soft God and thou wert wont to rest: "the soft God" is Cupid; "wert" is singular either by attraction from the word "thou," or because "the soft God and thou" is being understood as a singular subject.

OTHER FEMALE-AUTHORED ANONYMOUS LOVE POEMS

27. To―――― ["Love, deathless Love, is the most noble Sign"]. 1:14; Saturday, 18 December 1731. This is the first love poem to appear in *Caribbeana*; it is not given any introduction. The italics of the original have been normalized to roman.

Sign: "a mark of attestation (or ownership), written or stamped upon a document, seal, etc." (*OED*); this usage postdates by more than a century the latest example cited (1609).

Charge: "a thing or person entrusted to the care or management of any one" (*OED*).

28. Written at Midnight. 1:27–28; Saturday, 17 June 1732. Reprinted in Krise, 149–50.

Does on my Soul in mournful Slumbers stay: an error of agreement between subject and verb, like those in some of the poems assigned to the anonymous lady.

sad: "causing sorrow; distressing, calamitous, lamentable" (*OED*).

Sense: "the senses viewed as forming a single faculty in contradistinction to intellect, will, etc.; the exercise or function of this faculty, sensation" (*OED*).

Strings: nerves or muscular fibers.

Bays: fame or renown. This figurative expression, deriving from the leaves of the bay tree with which conquerors and poets were traditionally garlanded, indicates that the writer was already known for her poetry.

Frame: "applied to the animal, *esp.* the human body, with reference to its make, build, or constitution" (*OED*).

Traverse the Room out: go out of the room. Guskin plausibly emends the line to "traverse the Room, outwatch the dying Light" ("Not Originally Intended for the Press," 89 n. 33).

Thetis: a sea-nymph, famous as the mother of Achilles; the line means that the sun has not yet risen.

Prometheus: mythological figure punished for stealing fire for mankind by being chained to a rock and enduring daily visits from an eagle which fed on his liver.

Thus Love and Sorrow every Joy devours: error of agreement between subject and verb, perhaps because "Love and Sorrow" are being treated as a singular subject but also to enable the rhyme. "Feeds" in the next line follows suit.

29. To * * * * * * * ["Whene'er I leave thee, my unwilling Mind"]. 1:84; Wednesday, 13 December 1732 (dated 12 December in error). Though not explicitly by a woman, this poem resembles the other female-authored love poems in *Caribbeana*, and its emphasis in the final line on the writer's ability to love parallels similar declarations in, for example, poems 1, 5, 20, 27, and 34.

Imbrasures: embraces; a rare form of the word, not recorded with this spelling in *OED*.

30. Untitled ["Why pants my fondest tender Dove"]. 1:151–52; Wednesday, 25 April 1733. The first of a series of five connected poems, all printed in italics (normalized in this edition to roman). See the introductory comments in appendix A, pp. 122–24.

31. Untitled ["Your kind Example cures me more"]. 1:152–53; Wednesday, 25 April 1733.

Case: "condition, state" (*OED*); the medical sense, "the condition of disease in a person," is recorded from 1709 and so is also possible.

Strephon: like Damon, a name frequently used for a male lover in pastoral and amatory poetry, as in *The Epistles of Clio and Strephon*, the collection of letters, mostly in verse, by Martha Fowke and William Bond published in 1720. The poet addresses her lover by the same name in poem 34, the last one in this series.

————: as in poems 24 and 26, the dash indicating the poet's name occupies two metrical stresses.

32. Untitled ["I chide the Winds, and hate the Air"]. 1:153; Wednesday, 25 April 1733.

33. On naming Mrs. * * * *. 1:153; Wednesday, 25 April 1733.

Mrs.: until well into the eighteenth century this title was applied to unmarried as well as to married women.

O! treat my bleeding Heart with tender Care: the *Caribbeana* text begins with the word 'O' in large font and then repeats it in the normal-size italic font used for the rest of the poem, presumably in conformity with a house rule that the initial ornamental capitals of poems should be in roman. This edition therefore deletes the second 'O'.

34. Untitled ["When Oh! my Stars, when will ye join"]. 1:154; Wednesday, 25 April 1733.

Crook: traditional motif in pastoral poetry. Here, like "a Shade" three lines later, it indicates that the poet would gladly have accepted a humble life with her lover even if she had been much better born than he.

lazy: "favourable or appropriate to laziness" (*OED*).

35. An Imitation of Sapho. Written by One of her own Sex. 1:168–69; Saturday, 30 June 1733 (headed in error as Wednesday). This is an imitation only in a general sense. The italics of the original have been normalized to roman.

Sapho: see note to poem 14, "The Protestation," p. 140.

36. On Christmas Morning. Written by a Young Lady. 1:257–58; Wednesday, 2 January 1734.

Valentine: St Valentine's day.

From: away from.

wanting: lacking.

37. Untitled ["My longing Bosom wish'd to throw"]. 1:301; Saturday, 30 March 1734.

Clay: body.

38. To Mr. -------- on his having resolved to write no more. By Clio. 1:322–23; Saturday, 11 May 1734. "Clio" was the pseudonym of Martha Fowke. The identity of the addressee is unknown, but he may have been Aaron Hill or John Dyer. See the discussion on p. 33.

Reinforcement: help in persuading the addressee.

Apollo: patron of poetry and leader of the Muses.

flying Maid: Daphne, who prayed to her father Peneus to save her from Apollo's pursuit and was transformed into a laurel tree. The allusion is witty and mischievous, not only because of the change of gender roles, but because the myth was often taken to symbolize the victory of chastity over love.

Shakespeare: Martha Fowke's favorite poet. See *Clio*, 100–101, 111.

And feels the Pow'r: error of agreement between subject and verb, unless a misprint.

our Frozen Climate: England was traditionally contrasted with the birthplaces of classical literature, Greece and Italy.

charming: "using charms; exercising magic power" (*OED*).

thy Native Skies: probably a figurative expression linking the addressee with the classical sources of poetry; it is unlikely to indicate that he is literally a foreigner.

39. Untitled ["To *Aberglasney*, lovely Place!"]. 1:373–374; Saturday, 17 August 1734. Lines 1–6, 10–15 and 41–6 are reprinted by Richard C. Boys in *Grongar Hill: By John Dyer*, 29–30. The poem is indexed in *Caribbeana* with others addressed to Damon, but this seems an error arising from the use of the same name for the addressee. Damon, as a conventional name for a man in pastoral poetry, here refers to Dyer.

Aberglasney: birthplace and home of John Dyer (1699–1757) in Carmarthenshire, Wales.

their gentle Favourite: Dyer, who trained as a painter, also wrote poems, including several to Martha Fowke. Six of his poems were published in Savage's miscellany in 1726.

Mein: mien, "the air, bearing, carriage or manner of a person, as expressive of character or mood" (*OED*).

Herdlings: lambs. The fact that this very rare word also occurs in poem 23, assigned to the anonymous lady, may suggest that the same poet wrote "To Aberglasney."

Do with Tenderness inspire: error of agreement between subject and verb, probably by attraction from "Herdlings."

While the charming Strains he hears: the comma ending this line in *Caribbeana* has been emended to a full stop.

Happy Gronger! favour'd Brow: an allusion to "Grongar Hill," the poem for which Dyer has long been best known, first published in an early version in Savage's miscellany.

Cooper's Hill: the poem by Sir John Denham (1615–1669), published in its first version in 1642, which was often held to have inaugurated the eighteenth-century tradition of topographical poetry to which Dyer's poem belongs.

I retire with racking Pain: if the poem is by Martha Fowke, this may refer to her enforced withdrawal from Aaron Hill's circle in 1726 or 1727. See p. 34.

For I now the Bay resign: this indicates not merely social withdrawal but abandonment of her name as a poet.

Hymenial God: Hymen was the god of marriage; it was probably Fowke's husband, Arnold Sansom, who insisted that she leave Hill's circle.

fetter'd Clay: the body, in which the soul was traditionally thought to be imprisoned.

witty: perhaps "wise" as well as "possessing wit."

40. To ----------- ["From Love and Anger for a while set free"]. 1:392–93; Saturday, 19 October 1734. It is possible that this poem, which is printed with no introduction, is by the anonymous lady, because it is assigned to her in the Index.

arrant: "notorious, manifest, downright" (*OED*).

41. A Pastoral Song. 2:183–84; Wednesday, 26 January 1737.

AFTERWORD

1. Addison died in 1719, Prior in 1721, Congreve in 1729 and Lansdowne in 1735. Poem 12, "The Absent," refers to the South Sea bubble crash of autumn 1720, and this poem probably also dates from that year or thereabouts. An edition of Donne's poems, the only one between 1669 and 1779, was published by Jacob Tonson in 1719.

2. *Donne: The Critical Heritage*, 13.

3. Donne uses a nine-line stanza in "The Canonization," "The Flea," "The Indifferent," "Negative Love," "A Nocturnal upon S. Lucy's Day," "Song" (Go, and catch a falling star), "Twicknam Garden," "A Valediction: of the Book," "A Valediction: of Weeping," and "The Will." The other main difference between the anonymous lady's poem and all of these except "Negative Love" is that hers is uniformly in tetrameters.

4. See, for instance, the following poems in *Eighteenth-Century Women Poets*, ed. Lonsdale: Mary Chudleigh, "The Ladies Defence"; Sarah Egerton, "The Emulation"; Elizabeth Thomas, "On Sir J—— S—— saying in a Sarcastic Manner, My Books would make me Mad. An Ode"; and Anne Ingram, "A Epistle to Mr. Pope. Occasioned by his Characters of Women."

5. However, Phyllis Guskin suggests that the poem may have been written by Martha Fowke around 1710 and given at a much later date to the lover to whom she addressed the other poems of the sequence. See pp. 34–35 above.

6. *An Essay on Criticism*, 88–89, in *The Poems of Alexander Pope*, 1:249.

7. *The Poems of Alexander Pope, Imitations of Horace, with An Epistle to Dr Arbuthnot and the Epilogue to the Satires*, ed. John Butt (1939), 4:105.

8. *The Guardian*, ed. John Calhoun Stephens (Lexington: University Press of Kentucky, 1982), nos. 22 (pp. 105–7), 23 (pp. 107–9), 28 (pp. 122–24), 30 (pp. 128–30), 32 (pp. 135–37); Pope's paper is no. 40 (pp. 160–65). Congleton is cited in Stephens's note on pp. 625–26, to which this discussion is indebted.

9. *The Spectator*, ed. Donald F. Bond, 5 vols. (Oxford: Clarendon Press, 1965), nos. 102 (1:426–29) and 527 (4:380–81).

10. *The Poems of Alexander Pope, Minor Poems*, ed. Norman Ault and John Butt (1954), 6:45–47. The poem was first printed as an imitation of Waller in 1741. According to John Nichols, Atterbury's epigram was first published in the *Gentleman's Journal* in March 1692, with an introduction including the comment: "I never saw any thing more like Waller." See *The Miscellaneous Works of Bishop Atterbury*, ed. J. Nichols, 4 vols. (London: printed by and for the edi-

tor, 1789–1790), 3:296. Both Pope's poem and Atterbury's are included in appendix B.

11. See *John Gay: Poetry and Prose*, ed. Vinton A. Dearing and Charles E. Beckwith, 2:497–499.

12. The apparent solecism in referring to Jason as a Trojan is discussed in the notes to the poem, pp. 138–39.

13. *The Poetics of Sensibility: A Revolution in Literary Style* (Oxford: Clarendon Press; New York: Oxford University Press, 1996), 46. In chapter 5 of his book McGann discusses the three poems by the anonymous lady included in Lonsdale's edition of *Eighteenth-Century Women Poets* as early examples of the literature of sensibility.

14. "Against the Dead Poets Society: Non-Augustan, Non-Romantic, Non-Male Poets," *Halycon*, 15 (1993), 181–97 (pp. 194, 195).

15. "Not Originally Intended for the Press," 68–69.

16. For "herdlings," see pp. 33–34 in this text; the word "atom" occurs in poems 1 (line 30), 2 (line 9), 23 (line 14), and in three poems by Fowke: two in *The Epistles of Clio and Strephon* (pp. 45 and 64), and in "The Innocent Inconstant," one of her poems in Savage's miscellany (100).

17. Three in *Delights for the Ingenious*; eleven in *The Epistles of Clio and Strephon*; five in *A New Miscellany*, ed. Antony Hammond; forty in *Clio*; two in *Miscellaneous Poems, Original and Translated*, ed. Matthew Concanen (London: J. Peele, 1724); two dedicatory poems, one in *A New Collection of Miscellanies in Prose and Verse*, ed. Richardson Pack (London: E. Curll, 1725), the other in the second edition of James Thomson's *Winter* (London: J. Millan, 1726); nine in Savage's miscellany; and the one in *Caribbeana* assigned to Clio.

18. These statistics, especially the proportion of poems in pentameter couplets, are at odds with Guskin's claim that Fowke's acknowledged work, as well as the poems in *Caribbeana*, "demonstrate[s] a preference for octosyllabic couplets, or for a six-line stanza" ("Not Originally Intended for the Press," 68).

19. For example, in "A Description of a City Shower," first published in *The Tatler* in 1710, Swift famously parodied the two main variations allowed in pentameter couplets, the triplet and the Alexandrine. As he boasted in the 1735 edition of his works, later writers used them less. See *The Poems of Jonathan Swift*, ed. Harold Williams, 2d ed., 3 vols. (Oxford: Clarendon Press, 1967), 1:139–40.

20. Sir Thomas Browne, *Religio Medici and other works*, ed. L. C. Martin (Oxford: Clarendon Press, 1964), 112, 114. I am grateful to Gill Spraggs for pointing this out.

21. *The Poems of John Dryden*, ed. James Kinsley, 4 vols. (Oxford: Clarendon Press, 1958), 3:1170; *The Poems of Alexander Pope, The Rape of the Lock and Other Poems*, ed. Geoffrey Tillotson, 3d ed. (1962), 2:345–46. I am again indebted to Gill Spraggs, who not only directed me to Dryden, but also suggested that poems 17 (lines 9–12) and 20 (lines 1–6) seem to echo the same idea.

22. The pseudonym of the unidentified writer is Evandra; those of the unidentified addressees are Aurelia and Daphne. I wish to thank Christine Gerrard, who is preparing a new biography of Aaron Hill, for her help on this point.

23. *Clio*, 143–44.

24. Fowke discusses her marriage in *Clio*, 129. See also Guskin's comments in the Introduction to *Clio*, 29, 30–31 and 37–38.

25. See, for example, *Clio*, 100–101. Guskin mentions Fowke's passion for Shakespeare in her Introduction, 17 and 21.

26. *An Essay on Criticism*, in *The Poems of Alexander Pope*, 1:278 (line 346).

27. "To Aberglasney" is discussed on pp. 33–34 in this text.

APPENDIX A

Liberty of the Press: probably a double allusion, in part to Keimer's prosecution and conviction on a charge of libel, for which he was merely bound over to keep the peace (1:345–57), and in part to a series of articles entitled "Remarks on *Zenger's* Trial" in several issues of 1737 (2:198–221, 2:225–41). John Peter Zenger had been tried and acquitted in a celebrated libel case in New York in 1735. The first five articles were signed "Anglo-Americanus," a pseudonym for Jonathan Blenman, Attorney-General of Barbados from 1726 and Judge of the Vice-Admiralty Court from 1734, and the sixth "Indus Britannicus." Both writers took issue with the then highly controversial argument of Andrew Hamilton, Zenger's defense counsel, that "speaking and writing truth" could not be libellous. A footnote (2:200) indicates that Blenman's articles were reprinted in London (J. Roberts, 1738), though not that the same pamphlet also contains the article by "Indus Britannicus." See also p. 25 in this text.

Productions of these last: the reference is to the previous paragraph, which mentions contributions "from *private Hands*" (i.e., from private individuals).

not the only Author of the fair Sex: in addition to the verse represented in this edition, *Caribbeana* also includes poems by the dramatist Susanna Centlivre (1669–1723), the poet Elizabeth Rowe (1674–1737), and anonymous poems by women from Barbados.

a certain Gentleman, now in these Parts: not identified. See the discussion on pp. 25–26 in this text.

Duke of Rochefoucauld: Maxim 353, "Un honnête homme peut être amoureux comme un fou, mais non pas comme un sot." La Rochefoucauld's *Réflexions ou sentences et maximes morales* appeared in five successive editions between 1665–78, were translated into English by Aphra Behn and others, and were widely known in England and elsewhere from the late seventeenth century.

my CHAPEL: a footnote on 1:162 reads: "The first Printing-Press in *England* is said to have been set up in a Chapel in *Westminster-Abbey*; and from thence the Printing-Room has been ever since called a *Chapel*."

some of the politest Compositions: "polite" was a cultural keyword of the period, meaning "polished, refined, elegant" (*OED*).

a Man of Business: "One engaged in mercantile transactions" (*OED*). See the discussion on p. 28 in this text.

Pilgrim: the name of the Governor's house, as indicated by a footnote on 1:42. It had been built in 1710.

excellent Letters on Justice: refers to four letters signed "Philalethes" (1:229–32, 233–5, 240–43, 244–47). The name means "lover of truth."

Pity, Truth, Justice [. . .]: from Aaron Hill, "The Picture of Love," in *Miscellaneous Poems and Translations*, ed. Richard Savage (London: Samuel Chapman, 1726), 193–204, and addressed by Hill to "Miranda" (pseudonym for his wife Margaret).

Decline of Life: If this introduction is by Keimer, who was born in 1688, he would have been in his mid-forties at the time of writing.

Rape of the Lock: Canto 2, 17–18.

Letters concerning the English Nation: ed. Nicholas Cronk (Oxford and New York: Oxford University Press, 1994), 92. Keimer or his correspondent was very up to date in citing Voltaire's work, first published in 1733 in London.

Sir Isaac Newton: *Letters Concerning the English Nation*, 64.

those of a different Complexion: one of the very few references in *Caribbeana* to the black slaves on whose labor the colony depended.

your black Apartment: humorous phrase, used by Keimer himself, for his printing room.

Strephon: like Damon, a name often used for a male lover in pastoral and/or amatory verse.

a Gentleman to whom I am indebted: unidentified, but possibly Jonathan Blenman.

Authors of our Publick Misfortunes: the Assembly members ironically referred to in the *Gazette* as "the two Sofias" (i.e., the two wise men). The misfortunes arose from tax arrears incurred by many inhabitants on the advice of these two, an issue to which the *Gazette* gave considerable space.

Sir Richard Steele: "The *French* Faith Represented in the *Present State of Dunkirk*," in *Tracts and Pamphlets by Richard Steele*, ed. Rae Blanchard (Baltimore, MD: Johns Hopkins Press, 1944; New York: Octagon Books; London: Frank Cass, 1967), 269. The pamphlet was first published in 1714.

a late celebrated Performance: the reference is to Alexander Pope, *The Dunciad*, the first version of which appeared in 1728.

Boccalini, in his Advices from Parnassus: Traiano Boccalini, *Advices from Parnassus*, trans. John Hughes (London: printed by J. D. for Daniel Brown, 1706), 32. *Ragguagli di Parnasso* consists of satirical journalistic reports from the imaginary state of Parnassus, published by Boccalini (1556–1613) in two parts (Venice: 1612, 1613). The text in *Caribbeana* is a close paraphrase and at times a verbatim extract from the 1706 translation. A letter signed "Philanthropos" in an issue two weeks later (1:376–379) quotes a story from Boccalini (121–22) on the question of the double standard of sexual morality between men and women.

Intronati: members of an academy founded in 1525 in Siena.

Poems in chronological
order of publication

Index of titles and first lines